Bible Study Lab

# Praise for *Bible Study Lab*

We have had the privilege of knowing Chris Helterbrand for over a decade now. We count ourselves among his inner circle and very dear friends. One of the things that we have always appreciated about Chris is his diligent study of God's Word. Chris has done a great service for all of us as he has put in one spot his intentionality—a "how to" study of the Bible. Very proud of you, Chris. Proud to call you friend.

**Sandi Patty-Peslis and Don Peslis,** Grammy-award-winning vocalist, member of Gospel Hall of Fame, and author (Sandi), and pastor and author (Don)

I enthusiastically recommend Chris Helterbrand's book on how to study the Bible. I have watched Chris over the years learn how to study the Bible and seen how he almost immediately began to share this knowledge with others. His infectious enthusiasm to teach others what he has learned comes powerfully through *Bible Study Lab*. Chris will not simply tell you that you need to study the Bible; he will show you how. Get ready to be led on a journey by a person who has been where he is taking you.

**Dr. Cliff Sanders,** professor Emeritus, Mid-America Christian University

Reading and studying the Word of God is crucial and foundational to every follower of Jesus and their becoming all God wants them to be. This doesn't mean you have to be a theologian or Bible scholar. However, all of us should be students of the Bible. My friend, Chris Helterbrand, has written an excellent guide about how everyone who desires to, can study the Bible. There are some fundamental principles we can all follow to get to know this "manual for life," which God has given us. Chris has taken his unique and fun personality and woven it into this guide and made it so real, personal, and attainable. I recommend you get this resource and try it yourself—and even try it with a group. You'll find yourself laughing at his personal stories confronted with eternal truth in this life-changing book.

**Larry Harrison,** pastor of Worship Ministries,
Crossings Community Church, OKC, OK


Chris has made the Bible "user-friendly" as readers take simple steps suggested in the *Bible Study Lab* method. I predict the end game of the *Bible Study Lab* will have readers more informed and educated about both simple as well as complex portions of various books of the Bible.

**Marty Grubbs,** Senior Pastor,
Crossings Community Church, OKC, OK

In my Air Force career, which has spanned almost thirty years, I have learned a few things about successfully accomplishing a mission. You need a well-developed strategic plan and the right tools in your toolbox. Without those things, the adversary will most definitely have the advantage. For people of faith, one of our most critical missions is knowing all we can about the nature of our God and His will for our lives. Chris Helterbrand, a friend for four decades (and former college roommate), has provided both a truly thoughtful strategy and highly useful tools to expand our understanding of and deepen our relationship with our Heavenly Father. Chris walks us through a step-by-step process in *Bible Study Lab* using personal stories and humorous examples, which will make regular and consistent Bible study easier and more effective. He provides a framework that can take away the uncertainty of how to study so you can pursue what God wants you to learn. I highly recommend *Bible Study Lab* for anyone seeking a deeper understanding of the rich truths waiting to be revealed in Scripture.

**Colonel Don "Buzz" Kotulan,** Medical Service Corps, United States Air Force

# BIBLE STUDY Lab

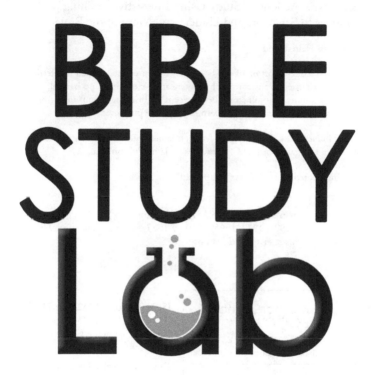

Develop New Actions of Study Using
**Interactive Training Techniques**
to See More and Understand More of the Bible

## Chris Helterbrand

NASHVILLE

NEW YORK • LONDON • MELBOURNE • VANCOUVER

# Bible Study Lab

## Develop New Actions of Study Using Interactive Training Techniques to See More and Understand More of the Bible

Published in New York, New York, by Morgan James Publishing. Morgan James is a trademark of Morgan James, LLC. www.MorganJamesPublishing.com

Proudly distributed by Publishers Group West®

**Morgan James BOGO™**

A **FREE** ebook edition is available for you or a friend with the purchase of this print book.

CLEARLY SIGN YOUR NAME ABOVE

**Instructions to claim your free ebook edition:**
1. Visit MorganJamesBOGO.com
2. Sign your name CLEARLY in the space above
3. Complete the form and submit a photo of this entire page
4. You or your friend can download the ebook to your preferred device

ISBN 9781636982328 paperback
ISBN 9781636982335 ebook
Library of Congress Control Number:
2023939026

**Cover & Interior Design by:**
Christopher Kirk
www.GFSstudio.com

**Morgan James PUBLISHING Builds** with... **Habitat for Humanity** Peninsula and Greater Williamsburg

Morgan James is a proud partner of Habitat for Humanity Peninsula and Greater Williamsburg. Partners in building since 2006.

Get involved today! Visit: www.morgan-james-publishing.com/giving-back

*To My Beautiful Wife who told me my written words had a voice. These words exist because of her words to me.*

# Table of Contents

# Foreword

As a career medical device rep, I've been instructed by dozens of medical companies, labs, and vendors in the importance of training, both for me and for my practitioners. Properly conducted onboarding, in-servicing, and didactic training is critical for several reasons but especially for two primary ones: safety and efficacy. Safety, because the life and limb of the patient could be at stake. Efficacy, because following the right protocol offers the best chance to achieve optimal outcomes. I was not only tasked with professionally representing my company, but I was also a steward and teacher of the best practices and appropriate use of its products and services.

On two separate occasions, with two different companies, Chris was my trainer and also taught my practitioners. Chris is a teacher of teachers. He is the consummate professional, one who has the unique ability to make extremely complicated protocols understandable to the entire team. He takes on an extremely difficult responsibility, makes it easy, and does so with kindness and compassion.

Prior to my career in the medical industry, I played football for twenty years. Five years at the Division 1 (D1) college level in the Big 10 and five years as a professional in the USFL and NFL. In sports, my medical career, and in my personal life, I have been blessed with incredible mentors. Truly great teachers, who have transformed the way that I looked at things and greatly improved my performance. Two that have had a uniquely profound impact are Joe Ehrmann and David Asscherick.

Joe Ehrmann (coach, author, ordained minister, professional football defensive lineman for thirteen years, the NFL's first Ed Block Courage Award Recipient and named by *Parade Magazine* as "The Most Important Coach in America") completely transformed my perspective, my heart, my mind, and my conduct as an athlete and a person, and equipped me with the tools I needed to achieve my goal of playing in the NFL.

David Asscherick (speaker/director for Light Bearers and ARISE co-founder and instructor) taught me, through the use of a rubric—"What is the point? Who is the person? How should I pray? Where in my life can I practice this? Promise of Power of the Holy Spirit!—to fully immerse myself in Scripture and understand and apply its transformative power in my daily life. I have also been blessed by other amazing coaches, teachers, family members, and others throughout my life.

Then along came Chris, with his *Bible Study Lab*. To say that Chris's method is transformative is a gross understatement. As an example, for the longest time I understood three verses in Matthew as Jesus using two different metaphors to teach the same thing. WRONG! With Chris's "Lab" method, a whole new biblical treasure was revealed to me. Chris innovatively applied the precise, hands-on, didactic medical training method to Bible study and the results are amazing!

At times, I must admit, that I had to reread paragraphs and even chapters several times to truly comprehend and apply Chris's method, but it was well worth the work. Chris teaches us a way to learn and apply God's Word in a new and enlightening way. His *Bible Study Lab* unlocks biblical power and has changed the way I will study Scripture forever.

**Kevin Kellin,**
former NFL player with the Tampa Bay Buccaneers

# Author's Note

For this book, you will need two things: this book and The Book (your Bible). Your Bible can be a print Bible or a digital/online Bible. That way, you can say you are reading two books. You're welcome.

*Bible Study Lab* was designed with my mentor and friend, Dr. Cliff Sanders. Dr. Sanders has pastored churches, taught at the collegiate level, written books, and taught more Bible classes than anyone I know. He has dedicated his life to the study of God's Word. He taught me how to study the Bible, and for this, I am forever grateful. He brought the skills of study, and together, we put the method together. We have discussed it, further developed it, and presented it for many years. It has been and will continue to be an honor to work with him on this project. He is my mentor, and he is my friend. *Bible Study Lab* would not exist without him.

I want to state upfront that everything I contributed to this book I learned from other people. I give the total credit for the content and writing of this book to God and to those who God put into my life. I am thankful for each person who has crossed my path and been a part of my development as a person and now as a writer. Some have been friends. Others have been business professionals. A few have been scholars. I am grateful for them all. This book is a collage of their knowledge.

My first hope is that my journey will shorten your journey to an increased knowledge of the greatest piece of literature ever written: The Bible. My second hope is that through the study of this literature, you will better see and know your Creator and Friend, our God.

This book is for anyone—believer or skeptic—who wants to engage with the words in the Bible. You might be a believer, looking to grow closer to God through his Word, and need a little help doing it. Great! These tools helped me do exactly that. You may be seeking or wanting to learn about God. You decided the Bible was a good place to start, but you aren't sure what to do next. That's great too. These tools can definitely provide direction as you investigate the Bible and a relationship with God. Sometimes I speak to people who have read the Bible but do not believe *because of what they read.* That position is understandable to me. I think many of us have been challenged by what we read at some point. Before I learned this method of personal Bible study, I could open the Scriptures and either get lost or feel confused. *Bible Study Lab* is designed to help overcome this confusion. Whatever your reason(s), I am glad you have chosen to read it.

I chose the title *Bible Study Lab* for a reason. I'm in the medical business, and for many years, I was a surgical implant representative. I routinely attended surgical cases with my products to answer questions about the product and its use. With some products, I programmed implantable devices during surgery. When things went smoothly, life was great. However, if the implant or equipment failed during the surgical case, many times, it was up to the representative to provide quick answers about the product. At that moment, your future business often depended on your ability to answer. If you ever wanted to do another case with that surgeon, it was imperative that you knew what you were doing.

In the medical business, we were trained to be prepared for this scenario. We attended many classes, but we also went into cadaver lab sessions and performed procedures ourselves, so we had at least some tiny hints about what the surgeon might be facing. In these labs, I gained so much knowledge as I used the equipment to practice abdominal surgery, orthopedic and spine surgery, pain procedures, and others. The classes provided information, but the real education—the application—came in the labs.

Let's view that in light of what we are doing here. We go to Bible classes. Maybe you call it Bible School. These are awesome. I wouldn't trade my time in Bible class for anything, but based on my medical history, I started thinking, "Where are the labs?" We need an interactive lab so we can better educate and prepare ourselves as we grow closer to our God through His Word.

The Bible Study Lab method can assist and enhance what you learn in a Bible class or from a sermon and move you to a deeper level of understanding and intimacy with God.

A biblical scholar, like Dr. Sanders, can use this method when studying the Bible. A Bible student, like myself, can also use this method to be successful in studying God's Word. We both use this method to learn more and that is really the point of the *Bible Study Lab* method. This book is not about what you know. I'd say it's about *knowing more*. My goal is to know more today than I did yesterday and more tomorrow than I do today.

Anyone can do it—scholars and students alike. I'm just glad you have chosen to start this journey.

*Chris*

# Method Development Summary
# Introduction

We will begin each chapter with a Method Development Summary. The summary will list the actions of the method with a focus highlighted section based on what was covered in the previous chapter. The summaries will allow you to see the method as it develops. The final Method Development Summary will describe the entire method and serve as a useful map to guide future Bible study.

## Method Development 1

This introduction will only list the summary categories.

- *The Basic Question* of Study
- Preparation for Study
- The Actions of Study

*Chapter 1*

# The Basic Question

*. . . and another day begins.*

It's early in the morning. It's so early that it's still dark outside. My eyes attempt to open, and I start to move, but that's just the involuntary movement of my inner time clock. I'm still asleep. I don't set an alarm. I'm getting older, and my body decides when it's getting up. It usually picks a time well before sunrise.

It's winter, so it's cold outside. It's cold in my house. My wife, code name "Nanook of the North," has turned the thermostat down so low that my refrigerator has become useless. It can't possibly keep the food as cold as my wife keeps our house at night.

I roll out of bed, grab my robe and slippers, and head to the kitchen to make the coffee. This frigid little walk begins the process of waking me up. I'm a little grumpy because I don't like anything about being cold. I realize it's manly to brave the cold. Whatever. I don't like it.

My eyes begin to focus as I enter the kitchen, and the first smile of the day comes to my face. Nanook, now known as "My Beautiful Wife," has prepared the coffee maker the night before. There is a piping hot pot of coffee ready to pour. I love her. She's the best. I grab my favorite cup, pour the coffee, and head to my office in our home. Those who know me know that something accompanies me and my coffee as we head down the hall. A foil package of goodness, otherwise known as a Pop Tart, is coming too. It happens every morning. Don't judge me.

I enter my office and flip on the electric space heater. A cozy flame-looking image appears, and the fan blows warm air, heating the room nicely in a few minutes. I take a nibble of the Pop Tart, sip the coffee, and put my feet on the desk. I'm awake. I think to myself, "I love mornings. Time to open God's Word."

I open His words and wonder what God will teach me this morning . . .

I am drawn to God. Deep down, I think everyone is drawn to Him. Some may not know it or may be confused by it, but I believe every created being is drawn to its Creator.

I am also drawn to the Bible. I love God's Word. Even when I didn't know how to study it, I loved hearing the Word presented well. I am intrigued by speakers who can uncover those seemingly obvious features or special details in passages that I have missed. I sometimes still wonder how some came to possess this depth of knowledge. A few speakers seemed to have had a special line to God.

I want to find that line. I wanted that knowledge. Getting it was another story. I had no idea how to do it.

## The Ole Flip and Point

Before I realized there was a process to Bible study, my study times were often frustrating. I didn't know where to start or really what to do to get the ball rolling. Many times, I employed "the ole flip and point" approach to Bible study.

You may be familiar with the flip-and-point Bible study method. The steps are easy.

1. Open the Bible.
2. Flip the pages until they somehow stop.
3. Close your eyes and point to a verse.

The next step is to open your eyes and tell God, "OK, God, I'm your student. Teach away." Inevitably, you have flipped and pointed to the middle of the book of Daniel and your eyes focus on a verse like this:

> "While I was observing, behold, a male goat was coming from the west over the surface of the whole earth without touching the ground; and the goat had a conspicuous horn between his eyes (Daniel 8:5)"

The next step of the flip and point method is to say to yourself, "That can't be right." You immediately shut the Bible. There must have been something wrong with your flipper and pointer. After all, what could God want to teach you about a floating goat with a misplaced horn? You try again. You apologize to God for the flip-and-point malfunction. You just know the process will work this time. Flip. Point. Your eyes open and this time the verse reads:

> "Now this is the inscription that was written out: 'MENE, MENE, TEKEL, UPHARSIN'" (Daniel 5:25).

Great. Daniel again. Why is it always Daniel? So you think to yourself, "Well, maybe this is what God wants to teach me." You determine that you are supposed to say the last four words of the verse. You close your eyes and try your best to pronounce "MENE, MENE, TEKEL, UPHARSIN." You say these words four or five times because something in your mind tells you that saying it once just won't work. You open your eyes and look around the room to see if maybe the Heavens have opened a portal of understanding.

Instead, the dog walks into the room with a look that says one thing: "Unless you want a mess, you better open the back door."

After quickly accommodating the dog, you try the flip-and-point method again. Maybe you end up in a different book, but each time you wonder why God would want to teach you anything in that verse. You end up trying to read a few verses but ultimately give up. You think to yourself, "I'll try again tomorrow . . ."

Sound familiar? I get it. I've been there. I was a card-carrying member of the Flipper-Pointer Club.

> *NOTE: Here is an odd point. As completely random as the "ole flip and point" method is, the tools contained in this method of personal study can help you*

*study a passage you find that way. I'd suggest picking
an entire book or finding passages to study through a
more organized effort, but you could "flip and point"
your way through the entire Bible utilizing these tools.*

When Dr. Sanders and I present the material of this method,
we typically start by asking the class what they are experiencing in their Bible study. What things go well when you study?
What do you enjoy about Bible study? How do you feel after
you study? We also ask about any challenges that are being
experienced. What keeps you from studying the Bible? How do
you feel when you are stuck in a passage? What do you do when
questions arise that you cannot answer? Write your thoughts on
these questions in the box below.

## A Perspective to Consider

If you have ever been frustrated and given up on study, this next section is for you. Consider the questions below.

Do you believe that studying the Bible is important?

Have others told you that Bible study is important?

We answer these questions with a resounding yes, but our answer creates a dilemma. In one corner, we know Bible study is important and others tell us it is important. In the other corner, we are left asking the following question:

**How do I start?**

That's a good question. How do you begin to study such an important manuscript? How do you personally engage a book that can affect your life so drastically? Beyond reading it, what do you do? I wondered about this for many years. Consider this next question:

**Have you ever been taught how to study the Bible?**

Dr. Sanders and I ask this question each time we teach this method as well. The response is usually around 10 percent. Think about that. Consistently, only 10 percent of the people we have asked over the last several years have ever been taught how to study the Bible.

The Bible is a historically accurate document containing multiple genres of literature. It is a complex book. This is a good thing in my mind. I'm glad I cannot read the Bible like an instruction manual one time and completely understand it without any other effort.

How boring would the Bible be as a daily tool if it were as easy to read as *See Spot Run?* God's Word is as powerful and useful today as it was the day it was written. It deserves our complete attention. It can direct our lives. It brings us hope, joy, and peace. It is one way that God speaks to us. These are just a few of the reasons that Dr. Sanders and I put together a method to study this incredible piece of literature.

As we engage in the method, there are a few questions we can ask to highlight the challenges of Bible study. Once we consider the impact of the answers to these questions, we get our first bit of direction, and it helps us move forward. These questions were powerful for me when I first saw them. Thankfully, I was immediately encouraged when I contemplated them.

This first question caught me off-guard. I love it because the answer immediately changes our focus and drives us to do things differently as we learn the process of Bible study.

### Is the Bible written to you?

Let me give you some details and questions to consider as you decide on your answer. You can pick any book of the Bible, but I'll use Ephesians as an example. The book of Ephesians is a letter the apostle Paul wrote that is part of the New Testament.

**Q: When was the book (letter) of Ephesians written?**

A: We can find out that Paul was killed in approximately AD 65, so we know Ephesians was written sometime before AD 65.

**Q: Who are the people mentioned in the greeting at the beginning of the book?**

Open your print or online Bible. Read the first verse and describe those mentioned in the box below.

A: "To the saints who are at Ephesus and [who are] faithful in Christ Jesus . . ."

**Q: Where do these people live?**

A: They lived in an ancient Greek city known as Ephesus.

## Summary

The letter of Ephesians was written close to two thousand years ago to a society of people who lived in an ancient city. So is Paul's letter to the Ephesians written to you? The answer is no.

Well, never say never, right? Let me say it in a different way. Unless you are a two-thousand-year-old Ephesian who lived in the city of Ephesus at the time this letter was written, this document we call a "Letter to the Ephesians" is probably not written to you.

If I am going to learn from a document that is not written to me, I need to set aside my perspective for a moment and consider it from a different point of view. To best understand Paul's letter to the Ephesians, I need to become that two-thousand-year-old ancient dude (or dudette) living in Ephesus at the time Paul wrote the letter. I need to walk in their shoes. I need to speak their language. I need to live in their communities and feel their way of life. This is not as hard as you may think.

It is important to get this permanently implanted in our minds because it changes the entire perspective of Bible study. I make it a habit to remind myself that the words I am studying are not written *to me*. They are written *for me*. They are applicable to me. They guide me. They console, lift, and convict me. The words are just not written to me, and this is OK. It doesn't change their effectiveness—only the perspective of study.

## The Basic Question

This knowledge leaves us with the final question that we will consider in this section. This question becomes our compass and guides us through our entire study journey. We will consider it from this point on in the *Bible Study Lab* method. We will call it ***The Basic Question***. I am going to boldly print the words ***The Basic Question*** each time I mention the phrase in the book, so we remember it is a specific question with a specific purpose in our study. Here is ***The Basic Question***:

**What did this mean to the original reader/audience?**

This is where Bible study begins. Once we understand the Bible is not written to us, this is the next natural question. If it is not written to me, who is it written to, and what did it mean to them? Imagine how this question by itself could impact study. I read a quote from an author explaining this concept. I have seen this quoted in different ways in many places and cannot determine the actual author. Suffice it to say, it wasn't me.

"A verse cannot mean to us what it could not have meant to the original audience." (Original author unknown)

I love that. How many times in the past have I read a passage and determined what it meant to me without considering at all what it would have meant to the original reader?

I would strongly suggest that you write down *The Basic Question* and position it in a prominent place that you can see as you study. Put it on your computer screen saver. Embroider it on your pillow. Write it on two thousand sticky notes and use it as wallpaper in your room. It's that important.

Depending on whether the passage is written or quoted language, the questions are:

What *did* it mean to the original reader?

What *did* it mean to the original audience?

At the beginning of this chapter, we asked, "How do I start?" My best answer is to pick a passage, realize it is not written to you, and begin the process of answering *The Basic Question*. That is the purpose of the *Bible Study Lab* method.

In the next chapter, we will engage the actual method. In the subsequent chapters, we will expand our understanding of the method and put it into practice. Put away your flipper and pointer. We are about to get our study on.

## Method Development 2

- **Begin study by recognizing the Bible is not written to me. This leads me to consider *The Basic Question:* "What did this mean to the original reader or audience?"**
- Prepare for Study
- The Actions of Study

*Chapter 2*

# The Actions of Study and Study Resources

*A quick word of encouragement . . .*

old on. We are about to take off. "Please put your tray tables and seat backs in the upright and locked position . . ." We will present many details in the next few chapters as we explain the *Bible Study Lab* method. It can be easy to become lost in these details. When you start to feel this, keep going. Eventually, the details will fade, and a process will begin to flow naturally. Hang in there. I promise you can do this.

The *Bible Study Lab* method begins with preparation and works its way into the actions of study. After we have described it, we will spend the next chapters engaging and performing these specific actions.

## Prepare for study. Clear your mind and pray.

We are all busy people. It is easy to pack something into every minute of our day. It can feel difficult to step away even for a moment. This makes prayer before study as vital as the spark plug in a gas engine. Prayer provides the spark necessary to get the study engine going during a busy day. That may sound a little cliché at first, but in full disclosure, I forget this too. I know I have a certain amount of time, and I feel the pressure of it, and sometimes, I just jump in. Consider this question:

**Why would I study God's Word
without asking God to be a part of it?**

I love the song "Turn Your Eyes Upon Jesus." The visual of turning my eyes upon Jesus when I study the Bible is impactful to me. When I turn my eyes on Him, I get a few minutes away from my busy day. It's just me and my King.

Before you begin your study, take twenty seconds, a minute, five minutes—whatever it takes for you to separate yourself from the busyness of life. Think of prayer as the transport to your little vacation destination with God.

Bible study is a partnership between you and God. Speak to your partner through prayer as you begin your study time. Continue this discussion with Him as you go. As you talk to God, ask Him to help you when you are in a passage that is difficult to understand. Thank Him when you find something special. Praise Him as He reveals Himself to you in His Word.

I suggest you write out your study prayers. I have found that writing down prayers provides great evidence of God's activity in my life when I find them later and reread them.

Sometimes my prayers are as short as "Help me, God" or "Teach me, God." Other times, my prayers are longer and more involved or based on what passage I'm looking at or what I'm going through in life.

If you need help slowing down to pray, use a breathe prayer. I use these many times. Here is how they work:

## Breathe Prayer

As you slowly breathe in through your nose, pray the words, "In this present moment, Lord . . ."

(Hold for a second)

As you slowly push the air out of your mouth, pray the words, "I turn my eyes on you."

(Repeat this process as many times as you need to focus on Him.)

Give it a try now. Close your eyes, breathe, and pray. Block all thoughts spinning in your head. Breathe in slowly as you pray the first line. Hold it for a second, then breathe out slowly as you pray the second line.

## ———— IT'S YOUR TURN. ————

Write down a prayer for your study today in the box below.

## The Actions of Bible Study Lab

Do you remember *The Basic Question* from Chapter 1? Write it in the box.

The actions of Bible study help us answer *The Basic Question*. The great part is there are only four actions in the *Bible Study Lab* method. There is obviously more to Bible study than these four words, but it all comes back to these four actions. I believe this makes study possible for anyone. I am proof of this. I learned these four actions and have developed and use them in my study. You will too.

This book is not designed to be an all-encompassing method of study. I don't know if that kind of book can even exist. It would certainly be a big book. This book is a starting point for your method of study. You will likely find the parts that work for you and further develop what you need. For now, start with these four actions. Spend the time to become proficient in these actions. As you put them into practice, your personal study and your method will develop.

The actions of Bible study are:

1. **Read**. Read the passage multiple times.
2. **Observe.** Determine features that capture your attention.
3. **Interpret**. Ask questions to answer *The Basic Question*.
4. **Apply.** Attach action and purpose to your study.

As you can see, the actions are easy to understand. It does take practice for these actions to fully develop, and we will begin to work on this together. The great part is that the actions of study flow together naturally. Keep the following summary in your head. It can help keep you on track as we work through the details.

> *When you read, you will naturally be drawn to certain features in the text. These are called* observations. *Document your observations and gather evidence to support and explain them. Interpretation is asking questions about the evidence, which leads us toward answering **The Basic Question**. Once **The Basic Question** is answered, application attaches action and purpose to its meaning in everyday life.*

This is essentially the *Bible Study Lab* method. In the following chapters, we will expand and develop skills in each of these actions of study. They will quickly become powerful tools. To do this, we first need some resources to use with the method. There are many resources available for us to consider. I will provide a little direction on how to find what you want and need to get started.

## Resources

As we briefly go through these resources, keep in mind that this is not intended to be an exhaustive list of resources. It is intended to be more of a starting point. You will probably change and add to your library of resources as you go. The resources provided in this book should give you a solid foundation to begin.

## Bible Versions

Many times, we are asked what version of the Bible to use. That's a complex question, and I have a very simple answer to it. All of them. I would suggest having multiple versions available when you study. This is extremely easy online.

I once attended a tour of churches in our city. I didn't really know what to expect, but it turned out to be a fascinating event. A bunch of people met at one location, loaded into buses, and went on a little journey to learn about five to six different churches. At each church, we met the church leadership and listened as they explained why they do what they do.

This was an eye-opening experience for me. I learned each church excelled at something. One church had a focus on worship, and they were great at it. Another was focused on liturgy. I didn't have a deep understanding of liturgy before that, but I saw the beauty of it when it was explained within the environment of that church. One church was exceptional at bringing in people who didn't know what a community of believers looked like. Another church was a teaching church. They were excellent at maturing Christians. The final church in the tour told the story of the Bible. It was amazing to see. The story of the Bible was portrayed on the walls, in glass—basically, everywhere you looked.

I learned a lot that day. I grew as a follower of Christ because of that tour. I learned that while I may not agree with all the theology of a church, I can appreciate and worship many places. Each church that day had something that helped build relationship with God through Christ. I would do a tour like that again, anytime.

Bible versions are a lot like that liturgy tour. I may prefer one version, but they all have something that helps me study. One may be focused on the language. Another version may be focused on communication. You might find another version that blends language and communication.

> *DISCLAIMER: I am definitely not an expert on biblical translations. I am also not writing this little section to tell you which version to use. I am writing to explain some of the differences. I have listed three versions of the Bible as examples only. If your Bible is not shown here, it does not mean I do not value it; it merely wasn't one I chose for the example.*

## There are basically three types of Bible versions:

1. Word-for-word versions.
2. Thought-for-thought versions.
3. Paraphrased versions.

Word-for-word translations take each word and attempt to keep the English word as close to the original language as possible. The NASB is an example of this. Thought-for-thought translations take the words of a statement or sentence and try to translate the thought. The NIV version is an example of this. A paraphrased version does exactly what it says. It takes the original language and paraphrases it to convey the idea. *The Message* is an example of a paraphrased version.

## Word for Word

Word-for-word translations stay close to the original language. Because of this, they can be "clunky" to read because, many times, it is not easy to communicate from one language to another. I remember trying to communicate in another language with a family that was visiting from a different country. Their daughter was fluent in both languages. She was talking with me and made an excellent point in our conversation. I looked at her parents and tried to tell them in their language that I thought their daughter would make a great attorney. Instead, I told them I thought their daughter would be a great avocado. The words were very similar. Their meaning was obviously very different. Never tell a man his daughter would be a great avocado. Just saying. Word-for-word translations seem to be great for study but a little harder to read.

NOTE: I list the NASB as an example of a word-for-word translation. Many of the online interlinear concordances use Strong's references in the form of a hyperlink in the NASB version. This makes it easier to gain the flavor of words when gathering evidence for observations.

## Thought for Thought

Thought-for-thought versions can provide a smoother reading experience, and help communicate what is contained in a passage that's harder to understand in word-for-word versions. In many cases, it appears to change just enough to make the passage easier to read, so I consult them alongside the word-for-word versions if I need to gain a little perspective.

## Paraphrased

I use paraphrased versions during the times I am reading the Bible and have trouble catching anything that is being communicated in the passage. We all have stumbled onto those long sentences in the Bible that stretch over multiple verses. It's like the writer forgot how to use a period. I can easily get stuck in these passages. When this happens, I use paraphrased versions of the Bible to gain a starting point. This usually gives me enough of a push to engage in the *Bible Study Lab* method and things start to happen in my mind. I have also noticed that paraphrased versions have a unique ability to beautifully communicate in the vernacular of modern language. I don't always stay with the paraphrased version during my detailed study, but the language can be so appropriate that I use it at times when I teach. In the past, when I ran into a long, difficult passage, I would generally move on to something else, thinking I would go back to the harder one later. That never happened, and I would lose the benefit of that passage. Paraphrased versions help with this, and I have used them to uncover amazing truths.

There are times I will read a passage in all version types, and it helps. If the versions differ in language, I have learned from people who know more than me to default to a word-for-word version because of its attention to the original language.

I am sure there are other reasons that explain how and why to use the different versions of the Bible. Just like the tour of churches, each of the Bible versions has something they do well. There is certainly reason to use more than just one version of the Bible in your study, and that is my point.

## A Brief Comment on the Reliability of the Bible

If we are going to base our life on the words of the Bible, we need to know it is something we can rely on. If it is going to be a compass that helps us know God, we need to know we can trust the words. This is a big topic that can be addressed in many other books. I will provide a few facts as references and point you in a direction to learn more on your own if you would like.

In full disclosure, I want the Bible to be true. I want there to be a God because my life story doesn't make sense without Him. I desperately need a Savior and believe it to be Jesus Christ. I can't imagine a life without the Spirit. The Holy Spirit has shown great capacity and desire to support, comfort, and direct me. I sincerely want and do believe that my life is sealed with a promise today and forever. Yes. I want this to be true and confess to you and God that I do believe this. You may not believe or may not be sure of what you believe right now. I just want you to know my personal perspective as we proceed.

I believe the Bible is a historically accurate document. I have read, listened, and learned from people educated on this matter.

Ultimately, you must decide what you believe about it. There are things in the Bible that make some people wonder about the Bible's reliability. The odd thing to me is that when we hear about or see something in the Bible that doesn't seem to add up, our brains immediately shove us toward thinking the Bible might not be true. I've done this more than I care to admit in the past. I would see something weird or controversial written or spoken about in the Bible and flip out a bit, without any effort or investigation on that matter whatsoever. The simple fact is that the Bible has never been disproven. It is heavily challenged, but it has not been proven false. I believe it takes more faith to *not* believe in the Bible than to believe in it.

There is also a huge amount of information called *attestation* that supports the Bible as an accurate document. If you want to investigate this, check out Lee Strobel's book, *The Case for Faith*. There is a video of this book available that can be bought online. At the beginning of the video, there is a section that does a pretty good job of getting you started on learning about the Bible as a reliable document. From there, you can find a plethora of material to learn more about the reliability of the Bible. Ask someone whose biblical knowledge you trust to direct you to other resources.

The focus of this book is not the reliability of the Bible but rather its capacity. *Bible Study Lab* does not exist to tell you what to believe. It's more about finding the evidence to formulate what you believe as you further your relationship with God through Bible study. We all have doubts. I firmly believe Bible study can help address these doubts, but it takes time and effort. Jesus spoke practical words, recorded in the book of Matthew, that address the use of the intelligence we have been given.

> "Ask, and it will be given to you; seek, and you will find; knock, and it will be opened to you. For everyone who asks receives, and he who seeks finds, and to him who knocks it will be opened" (Matthew 7).

This is Bible study. Ask, seek, and knock, and you will receive, find, and open.

## Bible Commentaries

Bible commentaries are great resources. Many of them contain introductions to the books of the Bible, which we will talk about later. I also use them to gather information when I am stuck in my study and need a kick start. I just don't use commentaries as my study—in place of the Bible itself. I certainly use them many times to check my work, especially if I have stumbled onto something unknown or controversial. Please don't misunderstand what I am communicating. I think commentaries are extremely useful tools. I use them often. As with most things in life, the more you invest in the study of the Bible, the more you get out of it.

## Online Resources

I love online resources and use them every time I study. This is not overstated. I use them every time. I enjoy using a printed Bible, but when I dig into Scripture, I use digital versions and all the supporting digital resources. I have them on my computer and on my portable digital devices. To me, it's like carrying a vast library everywhere I go. As with the Bible versions, I do not recommend one online resource over another. They all have something to offer.

It is important that you find an online resource you can be comfortable and confident using. There are many good ones out there. Watch the tutorials provided on the specific resource websites and search online for videos that demonstrate how they work. This effort will not disappoint you; the process has helped me understand what I need. Some resources can be purchased, and obviously, they have benefits too. My advice would be to start with the free online resources and figure out what you need and want as you go.

## A word of caution

I would not recommend searching the internet alone for answers to your study. In other words, don't just "Google it." Search engines tend to be a bit too broad to be effective. For instance, I would not type the word "faith" into my search engine. The result would be a flood of options with more details than anyone could absorb from sources that may or may not be trustworthy. This can create confusion and open the door to misinterpretation. Look around for websites that have data you can trust. Look for names you know. Ask someone you trust what they use.

That being stated, there will be times when you must go directly to the internet for research. When I do this, I check my work carefully among multiple sources. If a resource shows something no one else is indicating, it may be an opinion. Bottom line: Spend time finding reliable online resources. They are not hard to find, and they will serve you well.

## Print Resources

You may prefer to use printed resources. You may have access to a printed library of biblical resources. That's a nice blessing. The same information is available as in online resources, and many people simply prefer to turn the pages in a book. As with online resources, it is important that you find the resources that you will be comfortable using. If you prefer printed resources but do not know where to turn to find them, I again suggest consulting someone whose biblical knowledge you respect and asking them which books they would recommend.

Either way, online or printed, don't expect to have everything you need in the beginning. I doubt this is even possible. It would certainly be expensive upfront, and it's likely you would invest in resources you later find out are not what you really want or need. Your resources will build over time.

 **Stop and choose your resource(s)!**

At this point, stop and decide if you want online or printed resources. It is time to find a resource you can use to begin the study process. You will need to use these resources from this point on.

If you need help with finding **online resources,** type **"Free Online Bible Study Websites or Apps"** into YouTube, and it will get you started. Watch the videos! They will help.

If you need help with finding **printed resources,** type **"The best Bible study resources"** into YouTube or ask others what printed resources they use. There are many good ones.

Please don't be concerned about finding the "best" resource. I have used many, and they all have given me what I need. I have my favorites and so will you. In general, I would consider having the following resources:

- Multiple versions of the Bible
- A Bible dictionary and or Bible encyclopedia
- An interlinear dictionary or a concordance and a lexicon
- A set of commentaries, which are available on most apps/websites and in print

Here are a few of the app/online resources I have used in the past:

- Bible App (YouVersion)
- Blue Letter Bible
- BibleHub
- Bible Study Tools
- Olive Tree
- Precept Austin

Once you have your resources in place, you are ready to move to the next chapter. Hold on; here we go . . .

Bible Study Lab

# Method Development 3

- Begin study by recognizing the Bible is not written to me. This leads me to consider *The Basic Question*: "What did this mean to the original reader or audience?"
- **Prepare for Study: Clear your mind and pray before starting any study. Choose the online or print resources you prefer.**
- **The Actions of Study:**
  1) **Read:** Read a passage multiple times.
  2) **Observe:** Determine features that capture your attention.
  3) **Interpret:** Gather the evidence to answer *The Basic Question*.
  4) **Apply:** Attach action and purpose to your study.

## Chapter 3
# Reading

*It feels a little weird writing about reading to someone who
is reading what I'm writing. If you are reading what I'm
writing, then you know how to read and are wondering why
I am writing about your ability to read. However, if you
have stopped reading what I'm writing and are now thinking
about what I wrote, then my writing has produced something
in your reading. At this point, you are not reading at all but
thinking or possibly writing. Then it occurred to me: maybe
you are thinking about writing on what I wrote so someone
else could read what you wrote about my writing.*

Have you ever read a passage in the Bible that seemed
like this? This is how many of Paul's letters came across
to me the first time I read them. I would not describe
myself as a prolific reader or researcher, for that matter. I
enjoy it, but sometimes I struggle with it because my mind can
wander, especially when I read. When this happens, my efforts

at Bible reading generally fail to produce the results I'm after. This chapter was included to help provide direction when reading the Bible does not produce the desired results. Consider this next example.

## Self-Driving Cars

We have all driven a car and arrived at our destination only to wonder how we got there. It's a little scary if you think about it. I guess you could say that self-driving cars have been around longer than we care to admit. When this unconscious driving occurs, we don't recall what turns we made or how fast we were going or the stop lights along the way. It's hard to even recall the route we took to get there. It's unnerving because we simply can't remember. We just know we arrived at the destination. Notice I said "we" in this illustration. I'm implicating you with me so I don't stand alone.

I have caught myself doing this in Scripture countless times. I almost deleted the words "countless times," thinking I was overstating it. In my early days of Bible study, I unconsciously read on auto-pilot more often because I didn't really know what I was doing or what I was looking for when I read.

I would suddenly stop reading and, like in the car, realize, "I can't remember how I got here." I just knew I was at the end of the passage. I remembered very little about the characters, what they said, or any significant message from the passage. I think this is part of the reason Bible study can be challenging. It certainly outlines the importance of reading with purpose. The following questions and answers helped me with my reading of the Bible:

# Question #1: How do I stay focused during my reading?

## Answer: Ask simple questions.

If you are like me, sometimes the ole brain needs a bit of a nudge to start working. There are days I really want to read and study, but life has my brain full of thoughts that have me distracted. Maybe I am reading one of those seemingly never-ending passages, and I feel lost. Maybe I just have a lot on my mind. Whatever the case, when this occurs, I can have trouble keeping focused enough to generate any real progress, and I end up reading on autopilot.

I have learned to ask simple questions about the text before I begin. These simple questions keep me focused and on task while reading. Here are a few possible examples—there are certainly more to consider, depending on what you are reading. Start with "who," "what," "when," and "where" questions. Here are a few examples of these questions. It is certainly not limited to these three.

- **What is the genre of the book I am reading?**
  The genres of the Bible include narratives like the book of Genesis, poetry like the Psalms and Proverbs, or letters like Paul's letter to the Ephesians. There is a difference between reading the flowing figurative language of poetry in the Psalms and the literal narrative language of Genesis. Letters generally have a point(s), so I look for them when I read the letter. Understanding the genre of what I am reading while I am reading it can help with focus.

- **Who is the author, and what do I know about him?**
  Knowing who wrote the book and a little about the author affords more context when reading and helps with focus. Over time, I noticed the writing style or similar language in other books written by the same author, and this knowledge helps my reading overall.

- **What is the context?**
  When was the book written? What's going on in biblical and even world history around the time this book/passage was written?

I don't necessarily answer all the questions each time, but a few generally provide the context I need. They also help to place me among the original audience. There are times the answers to these questions cause me to ask other questions. This keeps me further engaged in my reading and helps with the next step of observation.

*Personal Note: Let me expand a bit on what I've learned about those seemingly obscure, hard-to-read passages. First, since the moment I engaged the tools of this method, I have never*  *been disappointed when I have taken the time in a difficult passage. Not one time. In fact, I am noticing they are more time-consuming than difficult. We will talk about time in study later, but I can tell you if I spend the time and use the tools, the reward is always there. Historically, I would move past difficult, obscure passages, thinking I would get back to them later. Usually, I never did. It may sound a bit weird, but now I look for them. Long, difficult passages have become biblical treasure maps, leading me to beautiful and powerful truths that affect my life. Learn the actions of study and test this theory out. I believe you will see the same thing.*

## Book Introductions

Another way to gain focus is to read an introduction to the book you are studying before you read it. These introductions can be found in many biblical commentaries and provide a few simple facts to maintain focus while reading. Many times, I will read these introductions even if I am familiar with the information in them. It simply helps me stay on task as I read.

## Question #2: How many verses should I read to understand a passage?

### Answer: The unit of measure.

There is an interesting feature that should be pointed out as we read the Bible. We tend to read the Bible in small passages or single scriptures. The unit of measure in the Bible is *the book*. By the book, I mean one of the sixty-six books contained within the Bible.

Wikipedia defines a unit of measure:

> *A unit of measurement is a definite magnitude of a quantity, defined and adopted by convention or by law, that is used as a standard for measurement of the same kind of quantity.*

It is easy to think of individual scriptures or passages within a book as if they were the full unit of measure. In other words, we feel as if the passage or verse contains all that we need to understand what we are reading. I am not suggesting we stop reading single verses or small passages, but if this is all we do, it is possible to miss information that would expand our overall knowledge. Reading the full unit of measure, the entire book, is important. I would recommend doing this as much as you can. If you feel stuck in your study, perhaps the best thing to do is stop and read the entire book.

## Grammatical Pointers

At a minimum, I make sure I am considering the entire passage within a book as I read. I use what I call *grammatical pointers* to find the beginning and the end of passages. *Grammatical pointer* is a "Chris word," so don't waste your time looking it up. Grammatical pointers help direct me to the beginning or the end of a passage. Verses that begin with words like "For," "So," "But," and "Therefore" indicate there is more to the overall communication than the verse I am reading. There are certainly other words and phrases that can act as grammatical pointers.

Sometimes, finding the beginning of an overall thought or passage is as easy as looking for a verse that doesn't begin with an obvious grammatical pointer. In these cases, I look backward in a book until the grammatical pointers stop and read until they end. Other times, I need to poke around a little more in the book to find out where a passage begins and ends. It is usually pretty easy to figure out with a little practice.

Ephesians 6:10–17 is a great example of this:

"Finally, be strong in the Lord and in the strength of His might. Put on the full armor of God, so that you will be able to stand firm against the schemes of the devil. For our struggle is not against flesh and blood, but against the rulers, against the powers, against the world forces of this darkness, against the spiritual [forces] of wickedness in the heavenly [places]. Therefore, take up the full armor of God, so that you will be able to resist in the evil day, and having done everything, to stand firm. Stand firm therefore, HAVING GIRDED YOUR LOINS WITH TRUTH, and HAVING PUT ON THE BREASTPLATE OF RIGHTEOUSNESS, and having shod YOUR FEET WITH THE PREPARATION OF THE GOSPEL OF PEACE; in addition to all, taking up the shield of faith with which you will be able to extinguish all the flaming arrows of the evil [one]. And take THE HELMET OF SALVATION, and the sword of the Spirit, which is the word of God."

## ——— IT'S YOUR TURN. ———

Locate the grammatical pointers you can find in this passage and list them in the box below:

There is a grammatical pointer, or at least a phrase that shows there is more to consider, in almost every verse. The word *finally* in verse 10 is a great example. "Finally," could indicate the beginning of a passage but also shows that verse 10 is the last point of a larger passage. As a side note, I believe it would be challenging to fully understand this passage without reading Ephesians Chapter 1. Again, reading the entire book before you study will produce more results.

## Question #3: How many times should I read it?

Answer: Consider this question:

> "How can I read a single verse, one time, that is contained in a book that was not written *to me* and hope to understand *The Basic Question*?"

Dr. Sanders describes the study habit of one of his scholarly colleagues. Before his colleague writes on a specific passage, he reads the book containing the passage fifty times. That is not a typo. He reads the book fifty times! Notice that he doesn't read the specific passage fifty times, he reads the *entire book* fifty times.

I tried to let you off easy by writing the sentence, "I realize you cannot read a book fifty times before you study it," but I don't want to disempower the significance of what this man did. It is truly enough to say, "The more you read it, the more you know it."

## Quick Review

Gather a little introductory knowledge before you read by asking/ answering simple questions to focus on the reading. Consider reading the entire book but definitely find the beginning and end of a passage before you read. Read it until you know it.

## Roll the Throttle Back and Look Around

Bible study is not just about repetition or reading the entire book. There is a paradigm shift that must occur in all actions of Bible study, especially reading. The shift is to reduce the impact of our schedule on our study as much as possible. This idea has made a significant impact on my study.

I love overnight motorcycle trips. There is something so relaxing about rolling the throttle back on the bike, releasing the busyness of life, and simply focusing on the scenery around me. My friends and I took a bike trip a few years ago. As we pulled out of my neighborhood, we had one plan. We were going to head south on Highway 81. That's it. We did not schedule anything else. We literally got on Highway 81, pointed the bikes south, rolled back on the throttles, and took off. It was an awesome trip. We didn't have any hotel reservations because we didn't know where we were going. And we had no idea where we were going to eat, what to expect, or what we might see. We had one thing on our minds—Highway 81.

Did I mention it was an awesome trip? If I listed everything we experienced on this trip, you would eventually stop reading. We grew as friends, ate amazing food, and met new people. I learned that on a bike trip, it's not how many miles you travel, it's how you travel the miles.

I suggest you do the same thing in your Bible reading. In Bible study, reading is like the bike throttle. Roll through the pages and let the scenery come to you. Reading is the plan. Set everything else aside. Set a timer if it helps, but during this time release yourself from work, from life, from everything except reading. It doesn't matter how far you get when you read. If you have a little more time, take your journey far. If your time is limited, let the journey develop over a few days. In the Bible, it's not how many pages you turn, but rather what you see as you turn the pages.

While on the bike, I notice things. The beauty of a tranquil farm setting or a flowing stream along the road might capture my attention. A neat country store with classic cars out front might grab me next. It can be anything. I am just out on the bike, getting to know what's out there. I think this is such a good example of reading the Bible.

I'm not suggesting we leave all schedules and order behind during study, rather we balance our expectations to allow Scripture the time to minister to us. Spend the time. Take the journey and get to know what is out there in the scriptures. This is the purpose of Bible reading.

## ——— IT'S YOUR TURN. ———
## TURN TO MATTHEW 5:1–11.
## READ IT ONE TIME THEN COME BACK.

How did it go? Did the passage engage you? Did you see anything? Let's try to add some context and see what that does for our reading. Before going any further, go to your external resources (the ones I mentioned at the start of this journey) and consider asking a few simple "who," "what," "when," and "where" questions about the passage. See if you can gain some context into the Gospel of Matthew. Remember, many commentaries have introductions that are helpful for this. Consider a few questions like . . .

**Who wrote the book? (Who wrote the Gospel of Matthew?)** It might feel like it, but this is not a trick question. Write your answer in the box.

## Now, who is Matthew?

Don't answer, "The guy that wrote the gospel of Matthew." I'm way ahead of you. See what simple information you might be able to find out about Matthew and his gospel in your resources and write it in the box.

## One more thing . . .

Read Matthew 5:1–11 again, but before you do, determine if you have engaged the entire passage. Look at the first five words of what we are reading:

"When Jesus saw the crowds . . ." (Matthew 5:1).

Crowds? What crowds? There appears to be more information to consider, but this is the beginning of the chapter. The only thing to do is to move back to the end of Chapter 4 and see what we can find out about this crowd Jesus saw. Start working your way backward from the end of that chapter to find the answer to *where* the passage begins. Look for the grammatical pointers. When you think you have it, list the verse where you think the passage might begin.

## Bonus Lab

If you were able to do this easily, "flip and point" to other parts of the Bible and practice finding the beginnings and ends of those passages.

I usually start studying this passage in Chapter 4, verse 23. Read Matthew 4:23–25 a few times. Roll the throttle back a bit and let the passage show a little scenery. List everything in verses 23–25 that indicates what Jesus did for the people in the crowd. Write this in the box.

As you read the last verses of Matthew Chapter 4, place your-self among the crowds. Imagine what it would have been like to experience this exact time in the ministry of Jesus Christ. Imag-ine God as Jesus walking among you and the rest of the people in this enormous crowd. If the Bible has taught me anything, it has taught me that when God walks by, things change. This time, God is doing more than walking. Imagine Jesus sharing with and teaching you. Imagine the excitement of Him speaking about His Kingdom and His willingness to share it with you.

If the excitement of what Jesus said wasn't enough, look at what he is doing. Jesus is also healing "*every* kind of disease" and "*every* kind of sickness" (italics mine). The word *every* leaped off the page at me. Pick a disease. It doesn't matter which one because He was healing them all. Now imagine being one of the people Jesus healed. A significant health issue has wrecked your life. This disease has stripped you of capacity. It has robbed you of opportunity. You tried to seek help, but healthcare is limited at best. You have minimal to no access to it, anyway. There are few options for your physical well-being, and your hope is fading. Then an incredible teacher trav-els through your area. You hear him speak. You begin to treasure His words and yearn for more. You are so mesmerized by what he says that, for a moment, you have forgotten about your health challenges.

Somehow, you end up in His presence. He turns His friendly, loving face toward you, and the unthinkable happens. You instantly feel better. You don't just feel better; you *are* better. This loving teacher has healed you, and your life is drastically changed forever. Your capacity is restored by His healing and your opportunities lie within His words. You would have followed him anywhere, and Jesus just gave you the physical and spiritual ability to do so.

Your excitement cannot be contained. You attempt, through tears and emotion, to describe your experience with Him to others and inadvertently become one of the crowd builders.

*And you're not the only one . . .*

## Back to Matthew Chapter 5

After experiencing a bit of life at the crowd level, you are now ready to read Chapter 5. Let's set it up as well. As the scene opens, Jesus sees the people. He turns to sit down on the mountainside and his disciples gather around him.

I love the language of the next phrase in the NASB in verse 2:

"He opened his mouth and began to teach them . . ."
(Matthew 5:2).

You are now part of this growing crowd that Jesus sees. You notice the incredible Teacher has stopped. He turns and sees the crowd that has formed and now follows him. He sits down and his disciples come in close. Everyone knows something is coming. It's why they are all there. Then you see him open his mouth. He is about to speak! Everyone in the crowd knows it and anticipates the first syllable of his incredible teaching.

## Dig Deeper

Think about the exact moment those in the crowd realize Jesus is about to speak. Hear as the silence falls across the crowds, stopping every conversation in mid-sentence. Watch as the people almost freeze in place as they anticipate the next words of this life-changing teacher and healer. Notice the focus of their eyes when they see him open his mouth to speak. The crowd collectively draws a breath and holds it so that nothing impedes His words from reaching them.

***It is a breathless moment in time.***

Now, slowly read Matthew 5:1–11 again. This is a passage you may know well. Take what you know about the moments before these words were spoken and allow the scenery of what happens next to impact you as you read. Read it over a few times and then come back.

Was your reading different this time? What scenery did you notice? Did something catch your attention? Write it in the box.

*A **Quick Tip**: Notice that we have not tried to answer **The Basic Question**. We are not ready for that yet. Fight the urge to read and quickly state what you think the passage means. At this point, we are just getting introduced to our passage—only just beginning our friendship with it.*

## ——— IT'S YOUR TURN. ———

Let's try another one. We won't dive as deeply into it, but it is a good one to practice with because it is a unique passage.

## Turn to Matthew 1:1–16. Read it and come back.

I chose this passage deliberately. What can we learn from reading this passage? There are obviously many names to read. Somebody begat somebody begat somebody begat somebody. It's easy to doze off or engage autopilot when reading all the names. If I notice a fly on the wall or a squirrel running across the yard, my study may come to a screeching halt. There are so many names that my brain just wants to move on. It is also easy for me to assume I get it. After all, it's just a bunch of names.

Forget the schedule and take your time. Roll the throttle back and look around. As I read, a few questions come to my mind. Why does this book begin with a bunch of names I can't pronounce? What could all these names mean to the original reader? Review the simple questions you answered about the Gospel of Matthew. Reread the book introduction in the commentary you chose.

Read the list of names again. Try it a few times if you can. Did you notice anything different? Write it in the box. We will address this action more specifically in the next chapter.

The general formula of this list is "so and so was the father of so and so, who was the father of so and so, etc." When we arrive at Joseph, the formula changes.

> "Jacob was the father of Joseph the husband of Mary,
> by whom Jesus was born, who is called the Messiah"
> (Matthew 1:16).

For obvious reasons, Joseph is not listed as the father of Jesus. Despite an immensely overwhelming patriarchal society that existed when Matthew wrote his gospel, this ultimately important list of lineage names from Abraham to the promised Messiah must include the female name of Mary. It simply cannot be completed without her.

Read through the names again. This time, see what other female names you can find. Write the names in the box below. If you want a little more "scenery," see what you can find out about these women and why they may have been listed in the lineage of Christ.

As we end this chapter, I will leave you with a great example from Dr. Sanders, which I watched unfold over a long period of time. It emphasizes my example of the bike trip and seeing the scenery.

Dr. Sanders taught a class at our church on the Gospel of John. *It took him eighteen months to get through the book in our class.* It took so long that we gave him a hard time about it. It didn't faze him a bit. I remember him saying at the end of multiple classes, "Well, we didn't get as far as I thought we would today." He wasn't concerned about the schedule at all. He just picked it back up in the next class.

**Why did it take so long for him to get through this study?** Was it because he wasn't organized? No. He's a biblical scholar whose organizational skill is impressive. Did he just have a bunch of extra time to study? No, he is in leader meetings, on Zoom calls, and in classes teaching more often than any man I have ever met. Was it because he wanted to see how long we would listen? Maybe. He's crazy that way, but his teaching is so strong, no one stopped listening.

We talked about this one day. The study of the Gospel of John took eighteen months because that is how long it took. In other words, a schedule didn't dictate the length of time in this material; the scriptures did. As Dr. Sanders read and studied, the passages kept giving. The more it gave to him, the more he gave to us in the class.

This is a great example of how slowing down can provide such great study benefits. I cannot imagine the knowledge loss that would have occurred if he had stuck to a schedule in the Gospel of John. A six-week course, or even a semester-long course, would have fallen short in its effectiveness. This is the case in study for us too.

As I considered the length of time Dr. Sanders spent teaching the Gospel of John, a question came to mind and pretty much stayed around until I answered it:

**If it takes Dr. Sanders, a biblical scholar, eighteen months to study and teach a book of the Bible, how can I significantly see the scenery of a book or passage in one or two days?**

This is a powerful question, one that has had a significant impact on me. I'm not assigning this to you. I'm suggesting there has to be a difference in the scenery I see in a few days compared to the scenery Dr. Sanders saw over all those months. It has caused me to move away from getting through the book and focus on getting *into* the book. It has been interesting to me to see how easy this is to do. It's not often we find something easy that is also beneficial, but eliminating schedule and merely staying in the passage longer is one of them.

In the next chapter, we will continue our journey toward *The Basic Question* and see what is possible *after* we spend significant time in the scenery of a passage. The next part is fun. You cannot do it wrong, so get ready to jump right in.

Bible Study Lab

# Method Development 4

- Begin study by recognizing the Bible is not written to me. This leads me to consider *The Basic Question*: "What did this mean to the original reader or audience?"
- **Prepare for Study:** Clear your mind and pray before starting any study. Choose the online or print resources you prefer.
- **The Actions of Study:**
  1) **Read: Read a passage until you have thoroughly observed the scenery in it. Consider the unit of measure and read the entire book if possible. At a minimum, find the beginning and end of a passage using grammatical pointers. Ask simple questions or read an introduction to the book from your resources to help with reading focus. Roll the throttle back, release the busyness of life, and let the scenery come to you. Take as much time as it takes.**
  2) **Observe:** Determine features that capture your attention.
  3) **Interpret:** Ask questions to answer *The Basic Question*.
  4) **Apply:** Attach action and purpose to your study.

*Chapter 4*

# The Concept of Observation

*A proud moment* . . .

n my first job out of college, I worked for a business equipment company. I sold business copiers and fax machines. As a new sales representative, fresh out of school, I made some rookie mistakes. One mistake I made is a good example of what *not* to do in business or in Bible study.

I was out making cold calls one day and walked into the building that housed my powerful learning experience. I noticed there were copiers everywhere. Unknowingly, I had walked into one of the largest copy centers in the city.

I was beyond excited to find such an opportunity. My head was spinning. Somehow, in my excitement, I managed to ask for the person in charge and was granted access to him. I thought, "Wow, this is the best day ever. I am so good at this!" I sat down with the office manager, introduced myself, and basically asked him if he would be buying any new copier equipment soon. To my utter amazement, he said, "Yes."

Selling is more about listening than it is about speaking. I learned that skill later. Before this poor man could say another word, I launched into an unrequested and lengthy dissertation on copiers. I also set up a second appointment to bring in my manager. I'm pretty sure the second appointment was given to stop my verbal onslaught of useless copier information.

When we arrived for the second appointment, I almost skipped as we were led to the man's office. I noticed, however, my manager was not skipping. I thought to myself, "Maybe he doesn't know how to skip. I will teach him later when we close this sale."

We met the man and began to chat. Thirty seconds into the conversation, my sales manager asked a question that changed it all. The reason my manager hadn't been skipping was that he had been noticing things about the account. Evidently, skipping and noticing things are not cohesive actions. He would teach me later. Touché.

My sales manager asked the man, "Are you a Xerox national account?"

The man said, "Yes we are. We have been a national account for fifteen years and are contractually obligated to buy from them." In case you are wondering, we didn't work for Xerox.

We spoke for a few more minutes and left. My business spirit was crushed. On the way out, I asked my sales manager how he knew they were a national account for Xerox. He replied, "Look around this place and tell me what you see." As I looked around, it was as if a portal of understanding opened before my eyes. Every single copier was a Xerox. There were Xerox marketing pictures on the wall. They had every Xerox giveaway known to mankind: pens, sticky pads, cups, you name it. It was all there. I'm pretty sure a few people even had Xerox shirts on.

Amazingly, I hadn't observed any of that. I just saw the copiers. It was one of the best educations I ever received. I learned abruptly to observe my surroundings as I spoke with my potential clients. Key word: *observe*.

## Observe

As I began to write about Bible study, this life lesson immediately came to my mind. I had to include my embarrassing moment in this book because it is such a good illustration of the word *observe*. I realized that reading the Bible without observing its surroundings is a lot like me walking into a Xerox national account and being oblivious to everything that pointed to it. Reading the words might give us a surface level of understanding. Observing all that is contained in and around the words will provide so much more meaning and understanding.

The Bible is a lot like that copy center. There are features that indicate what is going on if you take the time to look for them. Do you ever get those "hmmms" when you read the Bible? "Hmmms" are those audible noises that slip out of your mouth when you read something you don't quite understand. We all do this to some extent. They are created in our intellectual curiosity and develop naturally as we read.

Intellectual curiosity is a God-given ability that lives in us all. I notice something, and my brain subtly acknowledges it as something interesting or unknown. For me, that is when the "hmmm" slips out. Intellectual curiosity is the fuel for discovery. Consider what we have accomplished in the discovery of the universe or the human body. These accomplishments occurred because someone had a "hmmm" slip out and acted on it. Productive Bible study happens the same way. Allow your intellectual curiosity to take you to new places in the Bible.

The process of observation in Bible study involves documenting what you see that needs your attention. You cannot do this wrong because it is what *you* see. The trick is to document it. Write your observations down or type them into a computer. In my humble opinion, an observation has little chance of producing anything significant in study until it is documented. In the beginning, you might write down everything. That's OK. Over time, you will learn to discern what needs your attention. For now, just go for it.

## ——— IT'S YOUR TURN. ———

### Find Matthew 13:44–46.

Let's take a moment and see what can happen when we engage our intellectual curiosity. We will basically ask and answer simple questions that come up in the text as we read. We will explore some of the tools of observation in the next chapter, but the goal here is for you to see how study results can be produced by documenting what you see as you read. Revisit the questions for the book of Matthew. Consider reading the entire thirteenth chapter or even more.

## Read Matthew 13:44–46 multiple times.

The more you read, the more thoughts and questions will develop. Formalize them by documenting them in the box below. Don't judge what develops. The goal here is to write down what you see and then come back. Remember, you cannot do this wrong.

Matthew 13:44 and Matthew 13:45–46 are two short but separate parables from Jesus. Verse 44 is one parable and verses 45–46 are a separate parable. These parables teach two incredible but different truths about the Kingdom of Heaven. We will begin to establish the truths by answering questions that come out of our intellectual curiosity.

*A little reminder:* *As we ask and answer a few questions here, note that the answers I describe have been gathered through study done well in advance. I only offer my work here to show how the method can produce results. You will always want to do the research and gather the evidence before you provide an answer to* ***The Basic Question*** *on any observation.*

*Another little reminder.* *The purpose of this book is to illustrate the method more than to show my specific study results. The results I include could certainly be investigated more. My goal is for you to use them to get your own results.*

# Parable #1

Let's begin with the first parable in verse 44. Here are a few observational example questions and thoughts that came to my mind. Maybe you observed the same things as you read. We are just asking questions about what we observed when we read the passage.

> "The kingdom of heaven is like a treasure hidden in the field, which a man found and hid [again]; and from joy over it he goes and sells all that he has and buys that field."

## Q: What is the Kingdom of Heaven in this parable?

A: The first sentence in verse 44 states the Kingdom of Heaven is a hidden treasure. As treasures go, the Kingdom of Heaven would rank at the top of my list. There are no words strong enough to convey the value of the treasure in this field. I observe Jesus does not assign a value to the treasure.

## Q: Who is the man in this parable?

A: That is us. We are the man.

## Q: What is the man doing? List all the things the man is doing in the box below.

A: I observed these verbs in this passage:

1) The man *found* a treasure.
2) The man *hid* that treasure.
3) Out of joy, the man *goes* and *sells* all that he has and *buys* the field.
4) I also observe that the man has joy in these actions, but again, the monetary value of the treasure does not appear to require a definition.
5) Overall, I observe that once the man knows the treasure exists, nothing else matters. It reminds me of the movie *National Treasure*. Nicolas Cage is the lead character and seeks a treasure involving the history of his family. He puts everything on the line, including his life, in his quest for the treasure. The only thing that matters is securing that treasure. The man in the parable acts in a similar way.

## Parable #2

Now let's consider the second parable in verses 45–46. We will ask observational questions as we did in the first parable.

> "Again, the kingdom of heaven is like a merchant seeking fine pearls, and upon finding one pearl of great value, he went and sold all that he had and bought it."

## Q: What/who is the Kingdom of Heaven in this parable?

A: I observe that the Kingdom of Heaven has a different role in this parable. I found this very interesting. The Kingdom of Heaven is now a merchant.

## Q: What is the merchant doing?

A: The merchant is seeking fine pearls. It occurred to me to look for the verbs again. What actions does the merchant take in reference to the fine pearls? Write them in the box. Compare these to the actions in the first parable. What do you notice/observe?

## Q: Now for the really interesting question, who/what is the pearl?

A: You answer this one. Think about it and write it in the box.

**The awesome answer: You are.**

In the first little parable in verse 44, Jesus did not assign a value to the Kingdom of Heaven. I observed that this changes in the second parable where Jesus makes a value distinction. We are not just a pearl but a pearl of great value.

Contemplate this for a moment. Jesus has proclaimed that you are a pearl of great value. Let that sink in for a moment. He further states that His Kingdom seeks you because of your great value. I generally don't have issues understanding the value of the Kingdom of Heaven in the first parable. I do, at times, struggle with seeing *my* value mentioned in the second parable. According to the words of Jesus, if I believe the Kingdom of Heaven is a treasure hidden in a field, then I must also believe that I am a pearl of great value. You cannot believe one without the other. I observe that the words of Jesus dictate this.

These parables create an incredible relationship. Jesus wants you to seek the Kingdom of Heaven with everything you possess, but he doesn't ask you to do anything he hasn't already done for you. The verbs in these parables confirm it. Jesus Christ saw your value, sold all He had, and purchased your life.

### *You are the pearl of great value.*

What if tonight, as we drift off to sleep, we considered the fact that our God considers us to be the "pearl of great value"? How well would you sleep knowing that?

What if tomorrow, as our eyes open to begin a new day, we remember that the most important action is to seek the immeasurably valuable Kingdom of Heaven? How would this change your day?

We observed some pretty amazing features in this short passage. We did this by asking six simple questions in two short parables contained in three verses. There are so many more powerful tools that we will use in this method, but isn't it great to know that a simple question-and-answer session can provide so much detail?

As my friends and I traveled on that bike trip, the features of the scenery around us caught our attention. Sometimes, it was too incredible to miss, and we would turn in, get off the bikes and take a deeper look.

The same thing occurs in Bible study. If we minimize the impact of schedule in our reading, our intellectual curiosity will develop around the scenery of the Bible. The scenery produces a product we call *observation*. Documenting these observations captures our attention and gives purpose to Bible study. If we don't take this step, our study will often stop at reading. It really is that simple. Take note of things you see. Document things that make you go "hmmm." Pay attention to the things you don't know or understand and write them down. You'll be shocked by what this will produce.

In the next chapter, we will work with additional tools that will help us observe more and move closer to answering *The Basic Question*.

## Simple Tool for Study

To help me keep my Bible study organized, sometimes I take a piece of paper and fold it in half so it looks like a little book. On the front cover, I document my observations for the passage as I read. On the inside two pages, I keep all the evidence I collect about my observations, along with any rational and implicational questions and answers, which we will talk about later. On the back cover, I write my applications—the last step in our study process. When completed, you will have a nice little book of study. Organize and store these in a folder or scan them into your computer. You will be glad you did. Many times, I review old studies as I work on new studies. I'm always grateful for the information.

## ———— IT'S YOUR TURN. ————

Return to Matthew 4:23–5:11 again and see what observations you can find now. You've already read it a few times and even gathered a little context. Read it again. Start documenting the things you see or questions that come into your mind in the box below. Document things that make you go "hmmm." Pay attention to the things you don't know or don't understand and write them down. Read this passage a few more times. Each time you find something, document it in the box. This is great practice.

## The Ending of the Xerox Story

I wish I had been more observant in that copier center office all those years ago. My failure to notice all that was around me cost me some serious grief. When my sales manager and I got back in the car to leave that day, he sat down in the passenger seat and looked at me. He didn't say a word, and for a split second, I thought I was going to get away with being so ridiculous. Then he could not take it anymore and busted out in laughter, which lasted way too long, in my opinion. I couldn't even be mad at him because I was laughing too. How could I have possibly missed all of that?

## Method Development 5

- Begin study by recognizing the Bible is not written to me. This leads me to consider *The Basic Question*: "What did this mean to the original reader or audience?"
- **Prepare for Study:** Clear your mind and pray before starting any study. Choose the online or print resources you prefer.
- **The Actions of Study:**
  1) **Read:** Read a passage until you have thoroughly observed the scenery in it. Consider the unit of measure and read the entire book if possible. At a minimum, find the beginning and the end of passage using grammatical pointers. Ask simple questions or read an introduction to the book from your resources to help with reading focus. Roll the throttle back, release the busyness of life, and let the scenery come to you. Take as much time as it takes.
  2) **Observe:** *Engage the "hmmms" in your reading. As you read, your intellectual curiosity will point you to features that may need attention. An observation remains a random thought or question until it is documented.*

3) **Interpret:** Gather the evidence to answer *The Basic Question*.
4) **Apply:** Attach action and purpose to your study.

*Chapter 5*

# The Keys to
# Deeper Observation

I lose my keys . . . a lot. OK, every day . . . multiple times.

If you think this is a minor problem, I will tell you one of our friends built a beautiful dream home. In the plans of this house, they designed an alcove built into the wall called the "Chris Shelf." I am required to put my keys there the moment I enter their home because I have wasted a significant part of their lives looking for my keys when it was time to leave. So yes, I lose my keys a lot.

Thankfully, some wise soul came up with the idea of an electronic key finder. My wife bought me one of these finder systems for Christmas one year. I lost it. I really did. *I lost the finder system.* Never opened the package! I remember unwrapping it, but to this day, it remains lost. In my defense, I did find my keys that day.

I stated earlier that, at times, I struggle with reading and research, but effective Bible study cannot be accomplished without some of those two things. I sincerely enjoy reading and the research process, but I generally need a key—one I can find—to open the door and show me what's inside.

The nice thing is the keys of *Bible Study Lab* are pretty easy to find. Dr. Sanders and I have two keys we use for observation. They are more like master keys that open all the doors of study. We believe the use of these two keys will simplify the process of study for everyone. Learn to use these two keys, and you will go deeper in your study.

**The two keys are . . .**

**Grammar and History**

That's it. Grammar and history are the keys to observation and deeper study. Your observations will fall into one of the two categories. Our English and history teachers always told us that English and history would help us in life. They were right. You should call them and tell them you get it now.

**Why do the keys simplify study?**

Observations come naturally out of the multiplicity of reading. You cannot observe incorrectly because it is nothing more than what you notice when you read. The challenge is what to do with the observation. I see something. What do I do with it? Grammar and history address this challenge head-on. Once an observation is determined to be grammatical or historical in nature, we can engage the online and print resources to gather evidence about the observation. I was shocked to learn how simple it is to engage these resources, especially the grammatical resources.

Side Note: Observations can be *both* grammatical and historical, so don't be concerned if you can't decide where to go with an observation. In this case, use the resources for both keys.

If the keys are grammar and history, online and print resources are the vault. Find a grammatical or historical observation key and unlock the vault of knowledge. This helped me immensely in my own study.

We will begin with the grammar key. The history key will be addressed in a later chapter.

I spent my college days at Abilene Christian University. While there, I had a bumper sticker on the back of my car that read, "I are a college student."

Yes. I was *that* guy in college. As I wrote the words of that bumper sticker in this book, the grammar and spelling application on my computer flipped out a bit. It took notice of something in the sentence and highlighted it so I could investigate it. The computer doesn't like the use of the word *are* in that sentence because it's grammatically incorrect. In a similar way to a computer spell check, a focus on grammar in Bible study will highlight features that might otherwise go undetected. Think of the grammar key as a big, bright yellow highlighter for biblical understanding. It works very well.

## The Key of Grammar

Gathering grammatical evidence in observation is surprisingly easy. There are many features in grammar we could investigate, but we will focus on five concepts in this book:

1. Word definitions (terms).
2. Tense.
3. Mood.
4. Parts of speech.
5. Word study.

Using grammar has revolutionized my study of the Bible. This is not an overstatement. If anything, it is an understatement. I cannot imagine studying the Bible without this key. Grammatical evidence opens doors to incredible knowledge. This knowledge has translated into a deeper understanding of Scripture for me. Inversely, incorrect grammatical assumptions tend to close doors to understanding. This opens the doors to misinterpretation. Grammar in study is that important.

## Word Definitions

We will begin with word definitions, or terms, because they are the easiest. To help determine what a passage meant to an original reader or audience, we must consider what some words meant in the original language. It is not helpful to look up biblical words in an English dictionary. The words in an English-language Bible are written in English, but they are obviously English translations of other languages. Online or print concordances and interlinear Bible dictionaries are the tools to use when studying the words of the Bible. They address word definitions from the original language. I can't wait for you to see how quick and easy these tools are to use.

## Getting to the Grammatical Data in Your Resources

It is important to become proficient in finding the grammatical information in your resources. I am going to focus on the online resources because it is easier to describe in writing. I will describe this while using my computer, but it is just as easy on your smartphone apps. For this example, I will use BibleHub.

As a quick exercise, let's engage the resources for Matthew 6:12. From the BibleHub homepage, do the following:

1. Find the Book tab and choose the book of "Matthew."
2. Move to the Bible version tab and select "Strong's NASB" as the Bible version. I use this version because each word will display as a hyperlink that contains all the grammatical information related to that word. It's pretty awesome. Feel free to use whichever version you prefer.
3. Move to the Chapter tab and select "6." The website (or app) will take you to the sixth chapter of Matthew. Scroll down to verse 12.
4. In Matthew Chapter 6, verse 12, place your cursor over the word *forgive*, and a short definition will appear on the screen.
5. Click on the word *forgive*, and the full grammatical information will open in a new tab or window. Click on any word(s) in the verse and the same grammatical information will appear.

Look at all the grammatical information provided. There is the word from the original language, the part of speech, transliteration, phonetic spelling, and a generalized definition. Most resources will also have a speaker button that will pronounce the word in the original language.

I also like the "Word Origin" section below it, under the *NAS Exhaustive Concordance*. This illustrates the word(s) that are related to the development of the particular word you are researching. There will usually be one or two hyperlinks to give you more information about that.

Below the Concordance is the Greek Lexicon. You definitely want to get into the habit of checking your word in the lexicon(s). A lexicon will contain many, if not all, the scriptures that contain the word you are studying. Many times, they supply more specific information on how that word is intended in the specific verse you are studying. It is great information.

This is usually all in one place online. It will also be available for most printed material, although it may require the use of a couple of books to find both resources. Please use whichever you are most comfortable implementing. I use online resources because of the convenience. But they will both get the job done.

I mentioned most of the words in a verse or passage should be listed in a lexicon but maybe not every word. An example of this will be common words. Words such as *of* or *in* are used so many times, it would not be useful to see how it is used in every verse. You will probably not find every single word you look for in the lexicon.

Look carefully, though. Sometimes, it is hard to find the specific instance of the verse you want in the lexicon. It gets a bit tedious, but I am usually glad I put in the effort when I find it.

If the verse you are studying is not mentioned specifically, look at the generalized data or use the Word Study feature we will describe later. Bottom line: these word definitions will help significantly. Engage them and you will generally learn something you didn't know. I know I have.

Let's document the definition of the word *forgive* in Matthew 6:12. Look it up in your resources and write down the word definition in the box below. Write something in the box before you proceed. This is the action of gathering and documenting evidence for your observations. It is an important habit to form.

*The NAS Exhaustive Concordance* lists "apo" and "hieme" as two words that have been used to develop the word "forgive." The concordance states *apo* means "away from" and *hieme* means "send." Put that together and we get the flavor of "send away from." (NAS Exhaustive Concordance)

"Send away from." Isn't that a great description of the word *forgive*?

*Thayer's Lexicon* lists the verses where this word is used. If you scroll down a bit, you will find Matthew 6:12. The lexicon describes *forgive* as "to let go" and in verse 12, specifically, as "forgive."

The flavor we gather from an investigation of the word *forgive* includes "send away," "to let go," and "to forgive." When we forgive, we send something away. I learned forgiveness mimics the action of the archer with his arrow. The moment of forgiveness is like the moment the archer releases the arrow, and the arrow moves away from the archer. When forgiveness is given, the forgiven event begins the process of moving away from the one providing forgiveness. It doesn't mean the event didn't happen, but forgiveness releases the event and removes it from our presence so we can begin to heal. The more time that passes, the more the arrow moves away from the archer and the event moves away from the one who forgives. I found this to be a beautiful and helpful example of the concept of forgiveness.

This also provides me with a better understanding of Scripture and puts me closer to understanding **The Basic Question** concerning the word *forgive* as it is used in Matthew 6:12.

## ——— IT'S YOUR TURN. ———

Use whatever resource(s) you have chosen and look up the rest of the words in Matthew 6:12, writing the word definitions in the box. Remember *Strong's NASB* version of the Bible in online versions will typically provide hyperlinks to all the grammatical information.

## Keep It in Perspective

I am not a student of the Greek language. The closest I come to understanding Greek is when I order a gyro and baklava at the local Greek festival that rolls around each year in our city. I love this food.

It is important to keep in mind that when we use our resources for word definitions, we are not trying to translate a personal version of the Bible. I think of these definitions as more of the flavor of the word as I work to answer *The Basic Question*.

Additionally, there will be a tendency to want to look at all definitions of all words each time and find something "special" about each word. Occasionally, I do this out of curiosity, but overall, I would encourage you to focus on words that you feel are important to understanding the passage. You will become proficient at determining what these are over time.

## "I gave it my all."

I remember a time I took the definition research too far. As I was learning how to best use these tools, I chased after a word. I was studying Ephesians 4:31.

> "Let all bitterness and wrath and anger and clamor and slander be put away from you, along with all malice."

I was teaching a class on anger management and was confused by the use of the word *all*. I was confused because a couple of verses earlier, I had read Ephesians 4:26, which says,

> "BE ANGRY, AND [yet] DO NOT SIN; do not let the sun go down on your anger."

Verse 26 describes being angry but not sinning in anger. Verse 31 states to get rid of all anger. I was wondering how to harmonize these two verses, so I investigated the word *all*. The process I took to study this tiny word should end up in a comedy routine.

I used my online interlinear dictionary and looked up the word *all*. The Greek word is *pas*. The definition of *pas* used the phrase "including all forms of declension." This is where my brain took me on a senseless journey.

I had no idea what *declension* meant, so I had to look up the definition of that word. I did this in the English dictionary, which was appropriate because it is an English word. The dictionary defined *declension* as "the whole set of inflected forms." Great, now I had to look up the phrase "inflected forms." That definition mentioned something about the paradigm of a word.

I knew the word *paradigm,* but I had to make sure I understood how it was being used in the definition, so I looked it up too!

When I finally finished what became a ten-minute detour in my study, guess what I finally determined? Yep, you got it. *All* basically means "all." Paul was saying to get rid of all anger in verse 31. There is a great lesson on anger in comparing verses 4:26 and 4:31 in Ephesians, but I had to get out of the way before I could learn it. When I was done, I documented this process to remind myself that sometimes words simply mean what they mean. The lesson for you here is to avoid trying to find something special about every word in every verse. *All* of them.

## Two Additional Resources

I suggest gathering two additional resources. I didn't mention them before because I didn't want to create confusion. If you were to look at my phone, there is an icon for an English dictionary and an icon for a grammar resource. As I stated before, I would not recommend looking up Bible words in an English dictionary, but the resources use English terms that I occasionally need to look up. Additionally, it has been a few years (OK decades) since I attended a grammar class. The grammar resource has helped me remember the parts of speech, what modifies what, etc. It will be helpful to have both of these accessible.

## ——— IT'S YOUR TURN. ———

*SIDE NOTE: There is a goofy smile on my face as I write this next paragraph. I'm smiling because I know you are about to see how effective the key of grammar can be in your study. It forever changed my time in the Word. You may not be as proficient as you would like with the tools in the beginning. That comes with practice. Still, you will benefit at some level immediately, and that makes me smile. This is where Bible study becomes fun.*

## Look up a few of your favorite verses.

I will contradict myself and suggest that you look at each word in your favorite verses to give you some good practice. When you get to one, write the word and its definition in the box. The generalized definition should be quick and easy. Consult the lexicon to find out the flavor of the specific verse you are investigating.

NOTE: I have provided the entire next page for you to do your work. Save a little room if you can. We will also use this same box with the next grammatical features. Feel free to use a separate sheet of paper to do your work.

I hope you enjoyed this little exercise. Maybe you found something new about your favorite verse or verses as you investigated the word definitions. Let's see what else we can find.

## Tense

Tense is another one of those eye-opening grammatical tools. If you pay attention to it, it can produce some surprising results in your study. When you consider tense, you are determining if the language is referring to something in the past, present, or future.

I'm going to keep as many of the verses we work on in the book of Matthew as possible, but one of my favorite examples of tense comes from the book of Ephesians.

### Read Ephesians 2:1–8.

What is the tense of language in this passage? Is it past tense, present tense, or future tense?

Using the NASB version, what is the tense of the word *raised*? Write the word and its tense in the box below.

What is the tense of the word *seated*? Write the word and tense in the box below.

Stare at those two boxes for a moment. Consider both words and the tense of each. Read the passage a few more times and consider how the tense of the two words above impacts the meaning of this passage. Write your observations about this information in the box below.

*We have been raised.* This is past tense. *We have been seated.* This is also past tense. The two words are not something happening now. That would be present tense. They are not things that will happen in the future. That would be future tense. If you have chosen Jesus as your Lord, you have been raised and you have been seated with Him. Past tense.

I observed this passage places importance on where you sit. The tense associated with your seating is incredible to learn. How does the impact of already being raised and seated with Christ impact your day today? Determining the tense moves us closer to understanding **The Basic Question** in this passage.

─────── **IT'S YOUR TURN.** ───────

Go back to the favorite verses you have been working on. Go slowly. Read and consider the tense of what you are reading in each verse. See if the tense changes during the passage. Write the tense of the language next to the verse. Make a note of any place the tense of the language changes. Contemplate how the tense impacts the meaning of your verses. Once you have done this, come back, and we will move to the next grammatical key.

## Mood

Mood is my favorite grammatical feature. This chapter is dedicated to understanding the keys of grammar, and mood is part of that. We will describe *mood* here but engage it again and develop it further in the next chapter.

Did you grow up thinking that the words of the Bible were commands from God? I did. I never thought about it much. I just had it in my head that verses were commands. It is a fact that many verses are commands, but there are more verses that do not command. As an example, look at the first five words in the Bible. Where is the command?

> "In the beginning God created the heavens and the earth" (Genesis 1:1).

There is no command listed in these words. This is merely a statement that God created the heavens and the earth. Since there are more "non-commands" than commands, it is very useful to identify and determine the difference in the parts of language as we study it.

There are a few types of mood, but I am going to focus on two of them that occur most often in the Bible. Remember, this book is not intended to be an exhaustive set of tools but a way to begin. The two types of mood we will identify are declarative statements and imperative statements. Simply put,

## Declarative statements declare or state information.

"I have blue pants" is a declarative statement. The author or speaker is simply declaring the fact that he or she is in the possession of blue pants.

## Imperative statements describe commands.

"Go put on blue pants" is an imperative statement. In this sentence, the author or speaker is commanding someone to go put on pants and make sure they are blue.

It makes sense that we would study and apply a declarative statement differently than we would an imperative statement. In our communication with others, we do the same thing. We listen and respond to a command differently than when we hear others make a general statement. It is incredibly helpful to identify them properly as we study.

In the beginning, this can be a little confusing. I have listed a few scriptures to practice below. Are these examples declarative or imperative in nature? I'll start with an easy one. There is a giant hint in the words of the first Scripture. See if you can find the hint. Check the box of whether you think it is imperative or declarative.

"The heavens declare the glory of God; the skies proclaim the work of his hands. Day after day they pour forth speech; night after night they display knowledge. There is no speech or language where their voice is not heard" (Psalm 19:1).

☐ decarative

☐ imperative

"Do not let your heart be troubled; believe in God, believe also in Me" (John 14:1).

☐ decarative
☐ imperative

"The angel of the LORD appeared to him and said to him, 'The LORD is with you, O valiant warrior'" (Judges 6:12).

☐ decarative
☐ imperative

"Have I not commanded you? Be strong and courageous! Do not tremble or be dismayed, for the LORD your God is with you wherever you go" (Joshua 1:9).

☐ decarative
☐ imperative

## —— IT'S YOUR TURN. ——

Read Matthew 7:1–6 a few times. (By the way, that's an imperative.) In the box below, write down the declarative language and the imperative language in the phrases of this passage.

| Declarative | Imperative |
|---|---|
|  |  |
|  |  |
|  |  |
|  |  |
|  |  |

It's a good idea to note the mood as you study. As always, it is best to document it. You might also try this with your favorite verse box above. Write the word "Imperative" or "Declarative" next to the work you did earlier in this chapter. We will expand on mood in the next chapter.

## Parts of Speech

Determining parts of speech is a grammatical exercise that will often surprise you. These parts of speech are identified within the interlinear dictionaries when you click on the word. Determining the parts of speech generally serves as a wake-up call for me during my study. I can't tell you how many times I thought a word was a noun, only to find out it was a verb, adverb, or something else when I investigated it. This can be a game-changer in Bible study. It, too, significantly helps get me closer to answering *The Basic Question*.

—————— **IT'S YOUR TURN.** ——————

Just so you know, we will be starting and stopping a lot from now on. It is the only way I know how to make this book practical. On this stop, go back up to the previous box that contains your word definitions from your favorite verses. Document the parts of speech for each word next to the definition you provided. Some of the parts of speech will make perfect sense but pay attention. Depending on the verse, some parts of speech will surprise you. They become great observation anchors by themselves. Investigate them and you may be shocked by what you learn. Write what you learn about the part of speech.

I will use the *Blue Letter Bible* in this example. You know where to find it on BibleHub. Blue Letter Bible has a few nice screens pertaining to parts of speech that are helpful. As I said, I use many of these websites/apps in my personal study. They each offer a little twist.

From the Blue Letter Bible homepage, start at the top and do the following:

1. **Select the version.** I will use NASB20 in this case.
2. You will notice a box to type in the verse(s) you want. **Enter the verse** and **select "Enter."**
3. Blue Letter Bible separates out each verse. **Find your verse and select "Tools."**
4. You will notice each English word, the Strong's number "Inflected," "Root and Transliterated," and "Parsing." **First, select "Parsing."**
5. When you select "Parsing," a window will open, and you will see information about the parts of speech. The "additional resources" at the bottom of this window contain helpful information as well.
6. If you want to see the definition, select the Strong's number and a different window will open with all the word definition data.
7. There is also a lexicon for you to consult for specific definitions.

Again, use whichever resource you prefer and determine the parts of speech of the words in your favorite verses. Write this information alongside the word definition information in the box above.

## Word Study

There is another tool that adds flavor to understanding the words of the Bible. It is called *word study*. Word study is needed because sometimes the word is not mentioned in the dictionary, concordance, or lexicon, or those resources may contain only a limited definition that doesn't help much. Even if the word is shown in

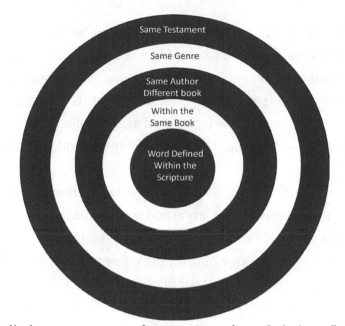

your dictionary or concordance, many times it is beneficial to determine how this word is used in other places in Scripture.

To understand how word study works, we will illustrate it using this red and white target. Your definition will be more applicable or specific the closer you are to the center of the target.

The goal of the bullseye is to define the word where it lies in the Scripture you are studying. We have seen how effective this can be using our interlinear and concordance resources. If you need more information, you will need to broaden your search for the word. If you need more understanding of the specific word you are studying, move out from the bullseye to the first white band of the target and see how the word is used in the rest of the book that contains the passage you are studying. In doing this, you can understand how the author uses the word in the context of that particular book. This provides the next closest evidence of how the word is intended to be communicated.

Sometimes the words are not used again in the same book. In this case, move to the next red band of the target and see how the word is used in other books by the same author. For example, the book of Ephesians was written by Paul. If I'm studying a word in Ephesians, but it is not used again in that book, I might look for the word in another book written by Paul, like Romans or Colossians.

If the word is never used again by that author, move out to the next white band of the target and see how the word is used in the same genre of literature that is used in that testament. Using Ephesians again as our example, the genre of the book of Ephesians is an epistle—or what we might call a *letter*. It was written by Paul. If I am studying a word in Ephesians, and I can't find an instance where it is used again either in Ephesians or other books written by Paul, I can look for the same word in another book that is also a letter. For example, I might look at one of the letters written by James or Peter.

Finally, if the word is not used again in a book of the same genre, move to the final red band of the target, and see how the word is used within the same testament.

I would suggest that the target example stops at this point. The New Testament was written in Greek and the Old Testament was written in Hebrew. While it is possible to make correlations between words in the different testaments, there are language differences between Greek and Hebrew that can complicate this process. Occasionally, there are words only used once per testament. If this occurs, and you feel the word is vital to your understanding, my advice would be to consult a person who has the education level you trust and ask for their assistance or their advice as to how to go about understanding the word. Word study is an effective ingredient in Bible study, and I have used it many times. There are times when it has even provided the only direction available.

## One Last Thing

In the next chapters, we will further engage the actions of study. We will use the two master keys to help us with our observations. As we proceed from here, it is easy to believe there is too much to accomplish for deep study. Dr. Sanders and I hear many people say, "I just don't think I can do this." I sincerely want to encourage you to stay with it as we proceed. Maybe the following example will help:

One of my favorite things to grill or smoke is chicken. Believe it or not, this little tidbit of knowledge will help keep the pieces of Bible study in perspective. Sometimes I have a plan when I grill, but usually, I improvise. I'll fire up the grill, put the chicken on, and then head to the refrigerator to mix my basting marinade. I'll open the door, look at all the ingredients, pull a few out, and "*whamo,*" I have it. I might pull out butter, olive oil, buffalo sauce, fresh lime juice—basically anything that might be in the ole fridge. I can literally open the door, close my eyes, and pull out a few bottles.

Here is the point: When I grill, I don't use *all* ingredients in the fridge *every* time, but I do use some of the ingredients each time. The result is usually very tasty. There are many ingredients that I could use in my marinade, but I can't possibly use them all. That would be frustrating and probably taste gross. The same thing applies to Bible study. Don't let the ingredients overwhelm you. The goal is to have them in your "Bible fridge" and use them as needed. I have never used all the ingredients in a single study. Like my marinade, I tend to pull out what I need and use those strategies for the passage I am studying. You can too. Over time, you will be able to determine which ingredients you need in your study to make that special sauce.

Hang in there! The further you go in the method, the more you will capture the process.

# Method Development 6

- Begin study by recognizing the Bible is not written to me. This leads me to consider *The Basic Question:* "What did this mean to the original reader or audience?"
- **Prepare for Study**: Clear your mind and pray before starting any study. Choose the online or print resources you prefer.
- **The Actions of Study:**
  1) **Read:** Read a passage until you have thoroughly observed the scenery in it. Consider the unit of measure and read the entire book if possible. At a minimum, find the beginning and end of the passage using grammatical pointers. Ask simple questions or read an introduction to the book from your resources to help with reading focus. Roll the throttle back, release the busyness of life, and let the scenery come to you. Take as much time as it takes.
  2) **Observe:** Engage the "hmmms" in your reading. As you read, your intellectual curiosity will point you to features that may need attention. An observation remains a random thought or question until it is documented.

      a. **Grammatical features, such as word definitions, parts of speech, mood, tense, and word study, are important.**

3) **Interpret:** Ask questions to answer *The Basic Question*.

4) **Apply:** Attach action and purpose to your study.

*Chapter 6*

# Matthew's in a Mood

I t's time to put into practice what we have been learning. We will engage Matthew 11:28–30 using the grammatical ingredients of word definitions and mood. Maybe you are like me and have worked through this passage many times. I had read, studied, and listen to presentations on this passage in countless sessions. I consider it to be one of my favorite passages. So, when I applied the ingredient of mood to my study of this passage, I was blown away by what I found. I could not believe I hadn't noticed it before. I can't wait for you to see this because while it does take time, the process isn't that difficult. The anticipation of knowing I can find or receive something keeps me in the Word. My goal is to be there every day. Let's start from the beginning of the method.

## Prepare for Your Study

Take a moment or two to step away from anything that may be in the way of your study. **Pray first.** Consider documenting your prayer. Write it in the box below. It doesn't need to be long or detailed. Just write what comes to mind as you are about to consider God's Word.

—————— **IT'S YOUR TURN.** ——————

**Read Matthew 11:28–30.** Read it slowly multiple times.

## Now read from the beginning of the chapter.

Set aside your schedule if you can and just take in the scenery around the words you are reading. Allow that intellectual curiosity to kick in. Remember, the unit of measure in the Bible is the book. If you have time, read the entire book up to this point. If not, verse 2 of Chapter 11 denotes the beginning of a passage. Start there and read as many times as possible.

## Observation (Matthew 11:28–30)

What do you see in these few verses? We will keep our focus tight initially and only consider verse 28 for the moment. Use the box to write down anything you notice in this verse. List any questions you need to answer to better understand it. Are there words in this verse that you could look up to find more flavor? Write them in the box as well.

"Come to me, all who are weary and heavy laden, and I will give you rest."

Ironically, our little friend, *all*, shows up again. I know you want to look it up. Don't go there. Remember my example? I've been there. "*Es no bueno.*"

Verse 28 is another example for me of how easy it is to read on autopilot, even with a single verse. I have read this passage so many times in the past that a cadence develops in my head as I read. I know these words so well; they feel as rhythmic as a familiar song. I have noticed I tend to miss opportunities to learn when this happens. It has become a bit of an indicator for me to stop and pay more attention.

In Matthew 11:28, are there words that need attention? Do any of the words drift by unnoticed? How about the words *weary* and *heavy laden*?

I have floated over these two words for many years because they almost seem redundant. I think that may be why it feels rhythmic to me. My Bible study experiences have taught me to pay attention to anything, anywhere that seems redundant. There is something to learn from repetitive words. This has worked well for me, and I have uncovered treasures, pieces of knowledge missing in my study.

## Word Definitions

Take a moment and look up the definitions of these two words in your resources and see what happens to these seemingly redundant words when we investigate them. Write them down, then compare and contemplate the definitions of *weary* and *heavy laden* in the box below.

*Weary* and *heavy laden* are different words in the original language, so if you think about it, it would be difficult for them to be redundant. The Greek word for *weary* is "*kopiaó*." It sounds like a great name for a coffee. It is actually a verb, and it means to "grow weary." The Greek word for *heavy laden* is "*photizo*." That sounds like an Italian sauce that goes over pasta. Maybe I'm hungry. *Photizo* is a verb as well, and it means "I load" or "I burden." These definitions help me see the flavor in the differing definitions of these two words.

Weary (*Kopiaó*) is Monday morning. I remember I had a job in the past that just wasn't a fit for me. I worked there for four years. I had owned my own companies for ten years before that and then went to work for a large, ultra-structured company. I was truly grateful for the job and worked hard, but I was just another ant on the anthill, and it was a big hill. I was used to running the company. Suddenly, I wasn't running anything. They ran me. I was miserable the entire time I worked there. I can't describe to you the depth of dread I had about Sunday evenings. I despised Sunday evenings because it meant Monday morning would soon be upon me, and I would have to subject myself to the business way of life that was demanded by the company. It made me weary. I had *kopiaó* running out my ears.

Heavy laden (*photizo*) is an entirely different concept. I get it too. My wife owned a boutique business. She rented space in a few of the local market locations in our city and sold women's fashions in them. Four times a year she sold her products in market shows. I would go with her and sell women's fashions for two or three days. I was oddly good at it. I don't know what that means, but whatever; I love my wife, so I did it. At these shows, we hauled the entire booth and all the products into the exhibit hall. We then spent hours setting set it all up. For the next few days, we worked ten-hour days during the show. Immediately after the show ended, we tore it all down, loaded it back into the truck, and drove home.

Some of this stuff was heavy, especially after a long show. I remember many nights hauling the equipment out to the truck. By the end of the evening, every part of my body hurt. The weight of the load had taken its toll on me. This is *photizo*. It is not pasta sauce. There is nothing tasty about it.

## Read Matthew 11:1–27.

As I read and consider the verses ahead of verses 28–30, I feel a tension in the words of Jesus. He loves the people, but some do not follow him. He offers some firm language that must have been hard for people to hear. For instance, listen to the words of Jesus in Matthew 11:24:

> "Nevertheless I say to you that it will be more tolerable for the land of Sodom in [the] day of judgment, than for you."

Suddenly, a few verses later, the language from Jesus changes drastically. As a side note, I observe that this model is seen throughout the many times Jesus speaks, and it is a good lesson for me when having difficult conversations. Jesus has just spoken difficult words. He follows them up with verse 28. Jesus says:

> "Come to me . . ." (verse 28).

As clearly as the tension comes through in the previous verses, the desire of Jesus for His people takes over the entire focus of the chapter with three little words: "Come to me." Jesus knows the capacity of their lives with Him and without Him. The evidence that supports this lies in the two words he mentions with his invitation, *kopiaó* and *photizo*.

## ——— IT'S YOUR TURN. ———

Let's broaden our scope as we engage the concept of mood in our study. Read Matthew 11:28–30 slowly a few more times.

Watch for the declarative and imperative statements. Determine whether the statements in this passage are imperative or declarative. Write what you observe concerning mood in the box below. Do the first three words of Matthew 11:29 form a command, or is Jesus making a statement?

The words, "Take my yoke . . ." form a command, so this statement is imperative in nature. Write your answer in the next box. Do this for the rest of the statements in Matthew 11:28–30.

"Come to Me, all who are weary and heavy-laden, and I will give you rest. Take My yoke upon you and learn from Me, for I am gentle and humble in heart, and you will find *REST FOR YOUR SOULS*. For My yoke is easy and My burden is light."

——— **IT'S YOUR TURN.** ———

Take a moment and document any other observations you notice in this passage in the next box. Use your resources and gather evidence on them as you can.

I'll expand on mood soon, but in my observational work, I engaged the definition of the word *take* in my online resource. Once I checked the general definition listed, I scrolled down to *Thayer's Greek Lexicon* contained in the link of the online resource I am using. This particular word is a great illustration of why lexicons are important. In this lexicon, the specific way this word is used in Matthew 11:29 provides a wonderful visual of how Jesus presents the yoke to us. The word *take* is the Greek word *airo*, but it is used in different ways in different scriptures. Note the differences in what is communicated in the different definitions presented in the lexicon:

> Definition number 1: "to raise up." This can mean to raise up from the ground or to elevate or lift up in the manner one draws up a fish.

If this was the definition intended for the word *take* in Matthew 11:29, we would need to pick up the yoke Jesus had for us *before* we could use it. If you look at the verses listed in definition number 1 in the lexicon, Matthew 11:29 is not listed. This is not the definition we are after (*Thayer's Lexicon*).

> Definition number 2: "to take upon oneself and carry what has been raised . . ."

If you look after this particular definition of the word, the fifth Scripture listed is Matthew 11:29. We know this is the definition of how this word is intended to be used in the passage we are studying (*Thayer's Lexicon*).

This definition is significant and emphasizes Jesus's intention to help us as we work. Jesus's illustration does not merely provide a yoke that is laying on the ground, waiting for us to go get it. Jesus actually prepares the yoke for use by raising it up for us. We have the easy job of simply walking up and accepting what He offers. Close your eyes. For a moment, visualize Jesus offering you a better way of life. All you have to do is step into it. It is ready for you and meant for you.

## How Are You Doing?

Hopefully, you followed the process and are ready for more. Don't be concerned if you are a little confused by it. It took me a bit to catch on as well. If you are not quite sure, please stop here and go back to the words in bold type—Prepare for Study—at the beginning of this chapter. Read through it and practice until you understand conceptually what is being done. Read over it a little more, and you will most likely have it. Here's the cool part: It gets better.

This chapter is a little shorter. We are going to add to it in the next chapter and add to the concept of *mood*, which we have developed here. In my study, the little flavor surrounding the word *take* admittedly lit my fire, and I wanted to know more. It was time to use the second key to open the history vault. Study goes to a higher level for me in the next chapter. We will combine what we have done so far with mood and fuse it with a little history. Our study is about to build dramatically.

## Method Development 7

- Begin study by recognizing the Bible is not written to me. This leads me to consider *The Basic Question*: "What did this mean to the original reader or audience?"

- **Prepare for Study**: Clear your mind and pray before starting any study. Choose the online or print resources you prefer.

- **The Actions of Study:**

  1) **Read:** Read a passage until you have thoroughly observed the scenery in it. Consider the unit of measure and read the entire book if possible. At a minimum, find the beginning and end of the passage using grammatical pointers. Ask simple questions or read an introduction to the book from your resources to help with reading focus. Roll the throttle back, release the busyness of life, and let the scenery come to you. Take as much time as it takes.

  2) **Observe:** Engage the "hmmms" in your reading. As you read, your intellectual curiosity will point you to features that may need attention. An observation remains a random thought or question until it is documented.

    a. Grammatical features, such as word definitions, parts of speech, mood, tense, and word study, are important.

    b. **The two keys of observation are *grammar* and *history*. Determine which key applies to your observation and consult the online or print resources to gather the evidence to support or explain it.**

3) **Interpret:** Ask questions to answer *The Basic Question*.

4) **Apply:** Attach action and purpose to your study.

*Chapter 7*

# Opening Doors
# with the History Key

M y mom was an extremely organized person. She was
also intensely committed to her projects. If she set
her intensity on something, it was going to get organized. She passed away in 2019, but her legacy lives on in one of
the last things that received her incredible intensity and organi-
zation. She produced something for our family that will forever
impress upon me the importance of history in Bible study.

Her last big project was a photo album set she put together
of our family. This was not a small endeavor. These albums are
full of pictures. Many of the pictures were from the days before
digital cameras and some were almost before cameras at all. It
has photographs and documentation of our family going back as
far as my great, great grandparents. She organized the project
and worked on it relentlessly until it was completed. It took her
many weeks, but she didn't stop until it was completely done.

That's how she did things. The result is a roughly twenty-volume album set. Each volume is thick, too, with multiple pictures on the front and back of each page. It's all perfectly and chronologically organized and noted with details. Like Matthew Chapter 1, it is the history of our family.

She gave me one of the albums for my birthday one year. It was my life in a book. She presented it to me as a birthday present, but she only let me look at it. When she left that day, the book, my birthday present, went with her. She said, "If you want to see your birthday present, you can come to my house." My mom knew my history with car keys. She also knew the value of the history she had put together.

Because of her great effort, people can come to know our family. They can see where we lived. They can know who we are and where we came from. In a sense, they can understand *The Basic Question* of our family.

The family history my mom put together helps me understand the need to gather historical evidence for the observations that come up in my study of the Bible. Historical evidence helps us see where people lived. We can know who they were and where they came from so that when we read passages that involve them, we better understand what they were experiencing.

Gathering historical evidence in a passage is generally more involved than the process of grammatical evidence. As helpful as it would be, there is not a single resource for historical evidence like the interlinear concordance and lexicons used to gather evidence for grammatical observations.

I would say grammatical evidence is given. Historical evidence is gathered. My mom gathered the evidence of our family. It took her a lot of time to gather her evidence. She enjoyed the process. The time it takes to gather historical evidence further emphasizes the need to slow down in our study. As I stated before, I am a slow reader. Research doesn't seem to flow for me like I see it flow in others. Like Mom, I genuinely enjoy the hunt for historical evidence. I have noticed that the more research I gather, the more I am drawn into the passage. As you look for evidence behind historical observations, you may not know where to look at first. Find someone you trust and ask them to give you some direction. Remember, I would avoid starting with simple Google or Yahoo searches.

I learned from Dr. Sanders there are three categories of historical evidence to consider. The categories are people, places, and practices. Understand the people, find the places, and learn the practices. Gather as much detail as you can in each category, and you will move closer to answering *The Basic Question*.

Ultimately, the only way to develop a skill in gathering evidence for historical observations is uh . . . well . . . to begin. The key for me has been to find one online resource or printed resource based on the passage I am studying. This can be an article, a video, a book, a map—really anything. I just try to find something. Your historical resources will expand as your topics demand. This is how your historical resource "library" will grow. I am still developing this and imagine I always will be. You can spend a few dollars in the beginning if you like, but the only real investment needed at this point is a bit of your time.

I'll give you one resource to get you started. You might look for a Bible encyclopedia, like ISBE. The *International Standard Bible Encyclopedia* is an easy place to begin. It is available in print or online versions. There are free versions of this on most websites and apps. They are generally older versions but still have good data to gather historical evidence. ISBE is certainly not the only one. There are many others that are just as easy to use.

The updated ISBE set will cost you some cash, but it is a good way to begin a library on a budget if that is what you want to do. I happened onto a hard copy, multi-volume set of ISBE at a used bookstore for less than $75. Admittedly, it was a good find, but they were out there (and still are!). By the way, used bookstores are pretty good places to find books on biblical history. They are worth a look.

> NOTE: Building an expensive online library or collecting books in printed form is not required. Through the free online sources, church libraries, borrowed books, and other options that are available, you can gather what you need, especially in the beginning.

**QUICK TIP!**

To illustrate the power of historical evidence in Bible study, let's go back to the book of Matthew. This time, we will combine the grammatical evidence of word definitions and mood and sprinkle them with a little historical evidence to see what happens.

## Go back to Matthew 11:28–30.

When we left Matthew's narrative of Jesus's words, we learned Jesus, the King, invites us to come to him for rest, and then He provides a yoke for us to go back to work. OK. We are going back to work, but what does it mean to take his yoke? What would "take My yoke" mean to the original audience? We need history.

## —— IT'S YOUR TURN. ——

Before you read what I found, take some time to see what historical evidence you can find about this passage. Remember the three categories of history to consider are people, places, and practices. Just give it a try. Do a little investigating and see where it takes you. If you don't have a resource, start with the ISBE, which I mentioned above. You might also try an online resource called Bible Study Tools or Precept Austin or The Bible App. Type the word *yoke* into your resource, then write what you find in the box below.

## Welcome Back!

I hope your quest for historical information was rewarding. Don't worry if it was not. This will develop with a little practice. I will share what I found. In my quest to learn more about the history of the yoke, I researched the idea of animals being yoked together. My research eventually led me to learn about draft horses. As I read about this topic, the passage began to unfold like a rose revealing its beauty, and I understood it at a completely different level.

## Just Horsin' Around

Here is what I found on my historical journey: I started investigating the concept of the yoke and eventually ended up at my state fair. Yes, even the state fair can be a historical resource. Our state fair has a draft horse competition. The horses involved in these competitions are massive and powerful. In the competition, two draft horses are yoked together to work as a team to pull heavily weighted sleds across a dirt track. The team that pulls the weight the furthest wins the competition.

*Hmmm. Yoked together to work as a team.* Seems like I read like that somewhere in the Bible recently . . .

To prepare for a pull, the handlers of the team walk the yoked teams around the stadium and prepare them to be positioned in front of a weighted sled. It's all part of the show, but the horses seem to get excited. As they are led to the sled, the horses stomp their hooves, kick up dust, and make snorting noises. It's a lot like my friends and me before a pickleball tournament.

A harness is attached to the yoked horses on one end. The other end has a metal ring used to link the team to the weighted sled. When the team is in position, the metal ring on the harness is dropped onto the metal frame of the weighted sled. A loud, distinct sound is heard when the metal parts slam together. The horses seem to know this sound because they respond instantaneously. The only word I could think of that properly describes this moment is *explosion*. The horses hear the sound, and their muscles "explode" with power, anticipating the weight. You can physically see this explosion of muscle manifest through the rippling under the skin. It may sound weird, but you can almost feel the power these teams employ when working together to pull the weight. If they have this at your state fair, go see it. It's worth the price of admission by itself.

When I got home, I further investigated the capacity of these draft horses, especially when yoked. It is astonishing.

I learned that one draft horse can pull 8,000 pounds. That is a significant weight. Imagine a few cars stacked on top of each other without any wheels being dragged across the dirt. That's roughly how much weight a single draft horse can pull. This is certainly an impressive feat, but let's take it further.

If a single draft horse can pull 8,000 pounds, how much could two draft horses yoked together pull? Maybe you did the math and came up with 16,000 pounds. Well, I learned from history that two draft horses yoked together can pull up to 24,000 pounds. Two horses yoked together have the capacity to pull three times the weight of a single horse!

I was beginning to see what the words of Jesus would have meant to the original reader. After providing rest, Jesus gives us an opportunity to work differently. He allows us to yoke with Him to handle the weight of life that we simply cannot handle on our own. I am reminded of the words of an old hymn: "What a friend we have in Jesus."

## Is There More?

In our study of mood in the previous chapter, we looked at the difference between declarative statements and imperative statements. We looked at the imperative or command statements in Matthew 11:28–30. Then we looked at the imperative, "Take My yoke."

## ────── IT'S YOUR TURN. ──────

Read the verses one more time and ask this question: "Did I find all the imperatives?" Congratulations if you did. I did not. There is another imperative after "Take My yoke." Write this imperative in the box.

Maybe you already knew this, but I had read this passage my entire life and focused only on the phrases "Come to Me" and "Take My yoke." The last imperative is "Learn from Me." Jesus invites us to go to him for rest. He then presents the command "Take My yoke," affording us the capacity to work a different way. The last command, "Learn from Me," is the power verse. And this power is exponential. Let's return to our example from the history of draft animals.

We learned that one horse can pull 8,000 pounds and two horses can pull 24,000 pounds. However, if you allow those same two yoked horses to *learn* from each other. Take a guess how much weight they can pull.

### 32,000 lbs.

Two horses yoked together and given the time to learn from each other can pull four times the weight of a single horse by itself! Not double, as we might assume, but quadruple the weight. I love this. I have taught this lesson many times because it is such a great example of how we can increase our capacity to move through the inevitable challenges of life. I actually came up with a title for this lesson, and it might be the best lesson title ever crafted. Wait for it . . .

"The Exponential of the Final Imperative" [pause for applause]

That title just preaches. It sounds like it belongs in a *Star Wars* movie. The beauty is the title is true. The final imperative in Matthew 1:28–30 is the power button for our lives.

I now understand what Jesus meant when He said, "Take My yoke" and "Learn from Me." Think of a time when life put its full weight on you. We have all had them. Maybe you are experiencing it now. Jesus knows what we face because He has been there. He knows better than we do the capacity we have with Him and without Him. If we are willing to accept His command, He will actually work with us. When we are yoked with Jesus, we learn that nothing can separate us from Him. That's also what a yoke does. Together with His power, we will pull through that which seems impossible. Jesus caps off his imperative statement with a beautiful declarative truth.

"For My yoke is easy and My burden is light" (Matthew 11:30).

Yes, Jesus. I accept Your yoke. Please remind me each day of how much I truly need to be yoked with You and learn from You so I never try to pull the weight of life on my own.

## Summary

Gather a little grammatical knowledge and sprinkle it with some historical evidence, and things start to happen. My mom's photo album impressed upon me the importance of history. I can learn about my family history any time I open the pages of those albums. It has helped me understand the importance of gathering historical evidence in Bible study. Yes, history requires more effort, but the results can be powerful. It must be included in the method because it produces such strong results. Thanks, Mom.

## A Little Encouragement while Gathering Historical and Grammatical Evidence

I took a different motorcycle trip with nine friends. We rode from Oklahoma City east to Bristol, Virginia, to travel down The Blue Ridge Parkway. On this trip, we experienced something that fits well with the concepts of observations in both grammar and history. Most of our riding was a lot like the trip I mentioned before—rolling back the throttle. Taking in the scenery. However, when we turned onto the Blue Ridge Parkway, our riding focus changed.

The Blue Ridge Parkway has a multitude of historical markers available to stop at and learn about some of the history of the area. Wanting the full "Blue Ridge Experience," we stopped at the first historical markers that came across our path. We got off the bikes, checked out everything, mounted up again, and rode on . . . about five hundred feet. Suddenly, there was another marker. We stopped there too. When we had investigated everything there, we found another stop just down the road. Stop. Look. Stop. Look. Stop. Look.

Evidently, someone in history performed some action every quarter mile on the Blue Ridge Parkway. After an hour or so of stopping at the consecutive historical markers, we figured out that if we didn't skip most of these things we were never going to get anywhere.

The same thing applies to Bible study. The point is to see the overall scenery and not every single piece of scenery (history or grammar) in Scripture. In the beginning, we stopped at each historical marker because we were concerned about missing something important. Over time, we realized we would experience more by leaving some experiences for another trip. In Bible study, initially, you may want to investigate every item. You may spin your wheels a bit while doing this. Eventually, you will realize where the stops need to occur.

Stay with it. You are doing great.

# Method Development 8

- Begin study by recognizing the Bible is not written to me. This leads me to consider *The Basic Question:* "What did this mean to the original reader or audience?"
- **Prepare for Study**: Clear your mind and pray before starting any study. Choose the online or print resources you prefer.
- **The Actions of Study:**
  1) **Read**: Read a passage until you have thoroughly observed the scenery in it. Consider the unit of measure and read the entire book if possible. At a minimum, find the beginning and end of the passage using grammatical pointers. Ask simple questions or read an introduction to the book from your resources to help with reading focus. Roll the throttle back, release the busyness of life, and let the scenery come to you. Take as much time as it takes.
  2) **Observe:** Engage the "hmmms" in your reading. As you read, your intellectual curiosity will point you to features that may need attention. An observation remains a random thought or question until it is documented.

a. Grammatical features, such as word definitions, parts of speech, mood, tense, and word study, are important.

b. The two keys of observation are grammar and history. Determine which key applies to your observation and consult the online or print resources to gather the evidence to support or explain it.

c. **Grammatical evidence is given. Historical evidence is gathered over time. The three categories of history are people, places, and practices. Watch for the categories as you read and observe. Understand the people, find the places, and learn the practices. Gather as much detail as you can in each category.**

3) **Interpret:** Ask questions to answer *The Basic Question*.

4) **Apply:** Attach action and purpose to your study.

*Chapter 8*

# Interpretation Using Implicational and Rational Questions

think of the times we moved. While packing up the house, I would inevitably find things I didn't realize I had. The excitement of finding these items usually derailed any progress I was making in packing. It was like Christmas. I'd start packing up an area and suddenly something would appear. It had been there the whole time. I just hadn't seen it. It might have been something sentimental from my childhood or something as mundane as a bag of items I forgot about from the hardware store. It didn't matter. I was always surprised when I found it.

Implicational and rational questions are a lot like this. Implicational and rational questions have shown me features in Scripture I've read—and even investigated—but have not seen. The more I engage these questions, the more I realize their importance. I can say that implicational and rational questions have provided some of the most jaw-dropping moments in my study. Consider the definitions of each question from Dr. Sanders.

| **Implicational Questions** seek to identify any conclusions drawn from the presence of what has been observed. This is usually accomplished by asking, "What can one infer or imply or suggest from the presence of the observed material?" | **Rational Questions** seek to determine the reason for the presence of what has been observed from the author. This is usually accomplished by asking, "Why—what reason or what purpose—is there for the observed material?" |
| --- | --- |

In the past, I never really thought to include implicational or rational questions in my study. For that matter, I didn't cognitively know to do it. As I think about it now, when I read, observe, and gather evidence, the interpretive actions of implicational and rational questions become the next natural step in the process.

*NOTE: Implicational and rational questions must be accompanied by grammatical and historical evidence. This is why we document*  *our observations and gather our historical and grammatical evidence first. Without evidence, it is easy to assign an interpretation to a passage that is more of a general idea or personal opinion than an actual implication from the passage. Many times while reading a passage, my mind wants to jump through the process and go directly to what I think. When I catch myself moving in that direction, I pull myself back and gather the evidence. Be cognizant of this in your study process. Don't steal the benefit of implication from your study by attempting it too early.*

The ingredients of implication and rationale are time and contemplation. Sit back and consider everything you have gathered and learned. Sometimes the answers to implicational and rational questions seem to fall out of my head. It can be that abrupt. I sit back and contemplate the observations and evidence. Then I ask what that information implies or why it is there and "boom"; the answer reveals itself and runs all over me. It's a fascinating process when that happens.

Other times, it takes extended amounts of time before I get to the answer. I may have other things competing for my attention, or I just may need to think about it longer. Ultimately, if nothing develops, I review all my work and even go back and re-read the entire passage. This usually helps. Just because I have read and studied doesn't guarantee me an immediate answer so don't always expect to see it right away. In my personal experience, the most powerful implicational and rational moments have come from passages I have spent the most time studying.

Sometimes I come up with an implication or a rational question and realize it doesn't match the work I have done in the passage. That's OK. I work through this in my mind and either edit what I have written or scrap it and start over. The anticipation that something is coming keeps me focused and on task during these times.

There are times when the implication or rationale is a simple little piece of info that I hadn't thought about in my study. I like these simple answers. They tend to roll around in my head all day, providing insight. Sometimes, these simple answers trigger answers in other passages. I have found this to be powerfully helpful.

There are also times when I consider all I have been studying, and suddenly, my mouth just hits the floor in amazement. These moments are usually followed by a thought in my head that goes something like this:

### "Whoa, where did that come from?"

These are amazing moments in Bible study, and I cherish every one of them. For me, it's as if God has reached down and said, "Check this out!!!" I am blown away when this happens. It can impact me for days. I wish I knew when God was going to do this, but that's about His timing and I am learning to trust it. I'm just glad it happens. The Bible is certainly not the only way God taps us on the shoulder, but it is absolutely one of them. These moments in Scripture energize me and provide an infusion of focus that helps direct my actions and thoughts for days. I can't say what this will do for you, but I am excited for you to see how powerful this can be so let's begin the process.

## ——— IT'S YOUR TURN. ———

Take a moment and consider the implication of the first three words in Matthew 11:28.

What do the words "Come to Me" imply? We have already done the work, so let's engage it and contemplate the impact. Try it yourself, first. Write an implication(s) in the box below. Review what we have done in the passage. Look at all the details you have written down and ask yourself what is implied from what you have learned.

I sat and thought about these first three words in Matthew 11:28 for a long time. Many thoughts ran through my head. The fact that Jesus stated "Come to Me" implies that coming to Him is possible. This is a powerful implication for just three little words. Jesus Christ, the King of kings, and Lord of lords offers an invitation and a path made possible by three simple words: "Come to Me." That this is even possible is staggering to me. I can come to my King. I can be with Him anytime I want. It is actually what He wants.

This is not normal from what I have learned about kings. But this King makes himself accessible to all His subjects, all the time.

I thought more about this. An implication came out of the declarative phrase "and I will give you rest." This implies the desire of Jesus, and it further confirms the implication I just mentioned. As the King of kings and Lord of lords, Jesus could have said, "Stop what you are doing, and I'll provide you rest." Jesus can certainly provide rest without commanding us into His presence. This is Jesus Christ, who once told a lame man to stand and walk . . . and the man stood up and started walking! He commanded a powerful storm to settle down, and it did! Our Lord instructed a dead man to come out of his grave, and Lazarus walked past the stone, alive as ever. If he can cause this to happen, I'm guessing he can speak a little rest into my life. But that's not what he does. Jesus says, "Come to me and *I will* give you rest" (emphasis mine).

As I thought more about it, I realized how different Jesus is as our King. He commands us to His presence so He can do something for us. Again, this does not appear to be a standard historical king-to-subject relationship. He is the one in power, but this King says, "Come to Me" and follows these words with the beautiful promise of "and I will give you rest." This implies a personal interaction for each person with Jesus Christ, our King.

*PERSONAL NOTE: I have noticed that others don't always become as excited as I do when I share what I have learned*

*from my study. That's OK. Please don't let this impact the significance for your spirit. When I find something in my study, my tendency is to want to share it with others. That may stir them, or it may fall on seemingly deaf ears. Think about it. When I share an implication, that person may not be familiar with the passage I studied. The implication may not catch them at that moment. In those cases, let the implication be a personal gift. I think it points out the significance of personal study. Study can produce results that can impact the spirit. Sometimes, it can be shared with others and lift the spirit of a community. Sometimes, it is an individual gift provided to the one engaged in the Word. It hits the target of effectiveness either way.*

## ——— IT'S YOUR TURN. ———

Now let's move to the command in verse 29. This time, contemplate the rationale behind Jesus's imperative statement: "Take My yoke."

Consult the definition of rational questions in the box to the right. When you are ready, stop and contemplate all you have learned. What is the rationale for Jesus's words, "Take My yoke"? Write them in the box.

**Rational Questions** seek to determine the reason for the presence of what has been observed from the author.

Oddly, the first thing that happened to me was that I found more implications. That happens a lot in my study. I look for one thing and find something to go with it. Once we have experienced His rest, the command is to go back to work. There isn't any discussion about it. He doesn't even take the time to say, "All right, you've had enough rest. It is time to go back to work." Jesus cuts to the chase and establishes the command, "Take My yoke." It is definitely implied that we are going back to work. The implication is that Jesus does not intend to leave us at rest.

"Take My yoke" also implies a different way of working. It implies a teamwork concept with Jesus. We are not left alone in our return to work. This time, we work with Him. I don't know about you, but I'm great with that plan. I need Him in my work every day.

I see the implication we are going back to work and that we will work another way, but what is the rationale behind why we are commanded to take His yoke? I found evidence in the verses prior to Matthew 28–30. In verses 16–27, Jesus basically outlines what happens to His people who are not yoked with Him and are working and learning apart from Him. Perhaps it is the reason they become weary and heavy-laden. Read verses 16–27 to see what you find.

Jesus understands our challenges and the way we respond to them. In verse 29, He does not make a request for us to consider working a different way. He knows where that path leads. Instead, Jesus supplies a specific command to work directly with Him. Specifically, the command is for us to work with Him *and* learn from Him. Based on our history of choices and actions, there is nothing else to discuss. The command contains what we need to move forward.

Take a moment to see what other implications and rationale you can find in this passage. You may not find any this time, but my goal here is for you to engage *the process*.

## Look at What We've Done

We read and studied a few definitions and a few imperative statements over a few verses from Matthew 11. As we took what we learned and contemplated the implications and rationale of their existence in Scripture, we began to understand what this passage would have meant to the original audience. The history and grammar of this passage produce a biblical snow globe that permanently captures this particular moment in time when Jesus saw where his people were and where they needed to be. It allows us to see into the beautiful character and intention of Jesus, our King.

## ———— IT'S YOUR TURN. ————

It's time to put it all together and summarize everything you have learned. But first, take a moment to pray.

Now, review everything you have read, everything you have documented and investigated, and everything you have contemplated and write it into a summary.

NOTE: Don't be concerned if you don't feel ready. Just try. If you can't come up with anything, go in reverse back through the process and read everything you have written. Feel free to edit, delete, or add as you go. Sometimes, I will reread the Bible passage a few times at this point too. Use more paper or type it into a document on your digital device if you'd like.

You will actually write two summaries. Write as much as you want in the first version of the summary. See what you can do with all you have learned in the next box.

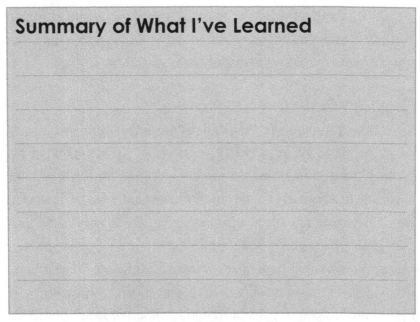

### Summary of What I've Learned

Once you have completed that, *summarize the summary.* Make it as short and concise as you can. Sometimes, that's a sentence or two or maybe a shorter paragraph.

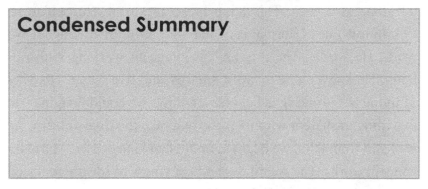

## Condensed Summary

### My Summary

In Matthew Chapter 1, Matthew details a lineage that confirms Jesus Christ as King. In Matthew Chapters 4–5, Matthew describes why people followed Jesus and the beautiful language He used to instruct them. Matthew Chapter 11 is another example of that instruction. Jesus, knowing His people, brings them in for rest and then commands them to take His yoke and learn from Him. He doesn't suggest it. His language is in the form of an imperative statement. It is a command. Perhaps He commands it because He knows the tendency of His people to exclude Him as they try to take on life on their own. I know I have done this. The implication of the words of Jesus is incredibly helpful if we take the time to understand them grammatically and historically. Jesus understands that, on our own, life tends to become wearisome and burdensome. Jesus knows this because he has lived it and has seen it in us. He knows we need rest from it, so He brings us before Himself and provides this rest.

In verse 29, the King's intention changes. The rest is over, and the King's command is for us to return to work. As our King commands us back to work, He informs us that, this time, we will not be working alone. Our King intends to work with us. He offers His yoke, and we take it, and we proceed to get the job done as a team. This King is willing to tie Himself to us to improve our performance. That's a pretty great King. If we work, He works. There is an advantage to working with our King. He knows how to work smartly and live better. His way of living and working is beyond anything we could imagine. He is willing to share it with us if we will take the time to learn. As we learn from Him, we begin to understand the benefit. His team concept works. The weariness and heaviness of life are replaced by a royal yoke that is light and easy.

### The Condensed Summary

Jesus knew that, on their own, His people were often impacted negatively by life. Jesus used the familiar example of animals yoked together to illustrate life as He intended. He directs His people 1) to Him for rest and 2) to be with Him for work, and 3) by providing private coaching lessons to engage in an unimagined life. The possibilities of life are endless when they are experienced through the exponential power of the last imperative offered by Jesus Christ.

*Woo. That preaches. Somebody pass a collection plate.*

# Wait for It . . .

## Guess what you just did?

If you wrote something in the *Condensed Summary*, you have answered **The Basic Question**. You read, observed, gathered evidence, and considered the implications/rationale of a passage to a point where you could document a condensed summary of your work. Do you feel better informed of what this would have meant to Jesus's audience on that day? That is the purpose of *The Basic Question*.

We accomplished considerable work in this passage and the work paid off. We took our time reading the passage. Maybe you read the entire chapter or even the entire book. We began with some simple grammatical definitions and identified the mood of the passage. We then gathered historical knowledge of draft animals and considered a few implications and the rationale behind what Jesus actually commanded.

Yes, there are multiple details to consider, but the process is somewhat natural. As I stated before, the details of the *Bible Study Lab* method will fade away and become an intuitive process over time, one you will augment and further develop as your own.

## One More Action to Go

We just have one more action in our study process. Before we move to the next chapter, let's take a shot at what we will learn next. The final action is the application. Let's attempt a quick and simple application. Matthew 11:28–29 shows that if we obey His commands, Jesus promises rest, teamwork, and coaching as part of a better life. Here is a very basic application to start:

> What if the next time the burdens of life felt heavy,
> I stopped for a moment to rest and reset my current
> thought process?

Take a moment and consider what might happen if you actually did this amid a challenging day. We will expand on the idea of this application in the next chapter, but for now, the act of focusing our thoughts on the rest promised by Jesus when life's work feels heavy is a pretty good start. Let's see what we can do to expand on this.

Bible Study Lab

# Method Development 9

- Begin study by recognizing the Bible is not written to me. This leads me to consider *The Basic Question*: "What did this mean to the original reader or audience?"
- **Prepare for Study**: Clear your mind and pray before starting any study. Choose the online or print resources you prefer.
- **The Actions of Study:**
  1) **Read:** Read a passage until you have thoroughly observed the scenery in it. Consider the unit of measure and read the entire book if possible. At a minimum, find the beginning and end of the passage using grammatical pointers. Ask simple questions or read an introduction to the book from your resources to help with reading focus. Roll the throttle back, release the busyness of life, and let the scenery come to you. Take as much time as it takes.
  2) **Observe:** Engage the "hmmms" in your reading. As you read, your intellectual curiosity will point you to features that may need attention. An observation remains a random thought or question until it is documented.

a. Grammatical features, such as word definitions, parts of speech, mood, tense, and word study, are important.

b. The two keys of observation are *grammar* and *history*. Determine which key applies to your observation and consult the online or print resources to gather the evidence to support or explain it.

c. Grammatical evidence is given. Historical evidence is gathered over time. The three categories of history are people, places, and practices. Watch for the categories as you read and observe. Understand the people, find the places, and learn the practices. Gather as much detail as you can in each category.

3) **Interpret: Contemplate the gathered evidence and consider the implications and rationale of your observations as you prepare to answer *The Basic Question*.**

4) **Apply:** Attach action and purpose to your study.

*Chapter 9*

# Application

My wife talked me into waxing my eyebrows once. Keyword: "once." I mean really, who does this twice? This tragic event happened one day as my wife was getting her nails done. We were headed to a movie next, so I was just sitting there in the salon, watching her and basically being me, when my wife suggested I get my eyebrows waxed. I was in a "go-with-anything" mood, so I said "OK . . . whatever. Let's do it." Immediately, I was escorted to a chair, provided a bottle of water, and even handed the remote to a TV showing some sporting event.

"Cool," I thought. "This is great!"

I sat down, and a nice wax application lady walked up, tilted my chair to a reclining position, and began speaking in a calm, sweet voice. As she was speaking, she placed this warm gooey stuff on my eyebrow. "That's nice," I thought to myself. At this point, I'm pretty sure I heard my wife giggle in the background, but I could be wrong.

After applying the goo, the nice application lady gently laid a tiny towel on top of the goo. I thought it was weird, but the warm gooey stuff still felt nice, so I didn't really concern myself with it.

Suddenly, I was attacked! The nice little wax application lady turned into Helga the Horrible and ripped my face off. She snatched that little towel off my eyebrow like she was stealing it. The pain was excruciating. The application of this process caused me to spring into action. My action was to yell. The word *yell* implies a manly action. My yell was actually a high-pitched scream, and it was completely void of manliness.

Ten Vietnamese women and my wife laughed and pointed at me. They had a great time. I did not. I'm done with the eyebrow waxing thing—forever. They got one eyebrow that day. The other one got away. I walked around with one pretty, but raw, eyebrow and one ugly, but safe, eyebrow. I did not care. I will never wax anything again. I don't even want to wax my car. The experience has left me mentally and emotionally scarred. Maybe even physically scarred, but the eyebrow grew back, so we'll never know.

The moral of this story is that *application causes action*. In my example, the application of eyebrow wax caused the action of my screaming. Hopefully, application in your Bible study will not cause screaming but some form of positive action in your life.

## Important Reminder

As we move into the final stage of the *Bible Study Lab* method, I think it is a good idea to review the self-correction in the method. It is not uncommon for me to get stuck—or so caught up in all the details—that I'm not sure what to do next. This is not a negative. It is just part of study. When I'm stuck, I have learned the answer is to back up.

I may put down the study for a while and come back later. This tends to clear my head and my process. When I come back, I work backward in the process and review the previous section. Chances are, if you do this, you will see more or gain additional perspective and be able to move forward. For instance, if you are looking for observations and are having trouble documenting anything, back up in the process and read more. We now know the more we read, the more the observations will spill out naturally. If they are not "spilling out," chances are, spending more time reading is the answer.

This also applies to the application process. If you cannot come up with an application, consider your answers to the implicational and rational questions and confirm you have answered *The Basic Question* in your summary. If you don't feel you have addressed it, look back at your observations and your grammatical and historical evidence. You may find yourself back at the reading stage. I do this process many times.

## So, What Is Application?

We spend time reading and studying, and the result is knowledge. Think of application as the way we spread this knowledge from our minds to the action parts of our bodies. Without application, Bible study is relegated to data collection. The critical step is attaching action to the data. If we fail to put action to our study, we merely learn what something meant to someone who lived a long time ago. It is important to answer *The Basic Question*.

Stopping at the answer, though, doesn't really cause anything to happen in our lives. The Bible is not written to us, but it is written for us. It is written for us to use in our lives. Application is what helps us use it. It is the personal action of a personal method of study.

"What if" questions are a great place to start when beginning to form applications. The words *what if* seem to send the brain on a journey to come up with an answer. I find it to be the easiest place to start. These questions look a little like this:

What if the next time _____,
I _____?

or

What if the next time _____
happens, I _____?

In the last paragraph of the previous chapter, I listed a basic application for our study in Matthew 11:28–30. I left this version of an application in a simplified form because I wanted to expand on it in this chapter. Let's now build on the application we started. Read Matthew 11:28–30 again. Contemplate what we have learned and then write down your first attempt at an application using the "what if" questions above. I provided my attempt below, but don't look at that now. Consider the "what if" for yourself. Jump back to the previous chapter and review (or read) what you've already learned if needed. Write your application in the box on the next page.

## What if . . .

Here is the application I suggested in the last chapter:

> "*What if* the next time the burdens of life felt heavy,
> I stopped for a moment to rest and reset my current
> thought process?"

We have a good start on the application, but let's see how we can build on it. "What ifs" help, but if I was left on my own, with no other direction to form my application, my funny little ADHD brain would have me creating completely obscure applications like this:

> "What if I jumped out of a plane while eating peanut
> butter and singing the song 'Yankee Doodle Dandy?'"

In case you are wondering, I'm not aware of any Scripture that would elicit such an application. I'm also aware that some of you will understand the possibility of coming up with such a ridiculous application.

Obviously, I need *focus*. Your brain may not take you down such extreme paths, but all of us could use a little help in creating effective applications. I'm grateful the words of the Bible can teach me today. It amazes me that a document written approximately two thousand years ago can impact me now—thousands of years after it was written. Application helps emphasize the contemporary capacity of the Bible. Without it, the Bible can feel like an ancient story.

## The Four Features of an Application

There are four features that will help form a useful application. Applications are:

- Specific
- Personal
- Attainable
- Measurable

These four features bring the focus I need to develop an action derived from my study. The key to that sentence is *from my study*. It's easy to come up with a general application to make changes in life. These four features provide the focus we need to form an application based on our study of a passage. We will describe each of them in the next few paragraphs.

### Applications Are Specific

Specific application is what allows this beautiful piece of historically accurate literature to be so much more than an ancient story. I can use this contemporary capacity of the Bible to generate authentic actions in my life. The specific actions have meaning now. To make an application specific, it must be tied to specific features I learned in my study of the passage. What specific feature in the passage can I implement in my own life?

## ─── IT'S YOUR TURN. ───

See what language you can add to develop a specific application. What specific feature from the study can you apply? What specific action can you come up with from that study? Write it in the box below.

Here is my attempt at a specific application from Matthew 11:28–30:

> "What if the next time I felt *unappreciated at work,*
> I stopped for a moment and focused on *what Jesus taught about rest and work in Matthew 11:28–31?*"

Compare this application with the first application I mentioned above. The phrase "I felt burdened by life" has been removed and replaced with more specific language—*I felt unappreciated at work* (see italics above). In this case, a specific application allows me to uncover what truly has me feeling burdened. Is it my job or is it something else in my life that is causing me to feel unappreciated?

Notice the addition of *what Jesus taught about rest and work in Matthew 11:28–31* (see the other italics above). This language directs me to a specific action in the text I have studied. I have taken the knowledge gained in my study and put action to it.

Like most actions of Bible study, there are times the development of an application takes a while to fully develop in my mind. You probably know what I'm going to say (and you'd be correct). "Roll the throttle back and forget the schedule." Allow the time necessary for this two-thousand-year-old document to bring out a contemporary action in your life. Write down the application and think about it. See if it captures what you learned. If it still doesn't develop, back up in the process and check your work.

## Applications Are Personal

Have you ever been in church and the speaker mentioned something that you felt really applied to the family member sitting next to you? You nudged your elbow into their ribs, didn't you? You know you did. I did too. Why is an elbow to the ribs the only FDA-approved action in this situation? Where did that church tradition begin?

Who was the first person to think, "Ya know what would help my family member gain perspective from God? Yep. The sharpest, most penetrating bone in my body placed into their ribs. That should help."

Applications are made by the person, for the person. This is the reason an elbow can't possibly be a tool for personal application. It is not personal to the person applying it. Injurious? Yes. Personal? No. Here is my proof: Have the following words ever been uttered by the recipient of an elbow during a worship service?

> "Oh, thank you so much for focusing on my faults during this worship service. Evidently, I failed to do this on my own. The precise placement of your elbow into my ribs was the kind but jolting gesture I needed. It has allowed me to see the folly of my ways. Bless you, my kind and considerate family member."

Uh, no. I have never said this, and I have been "elbowed" many times in church. Before I start a family argument, let's just remember the best applications are generated by the person, for the person.

I teach Bible classes because it helps me stay in the Word. Sometimes I catch myself using lesson preparation as my personal Bible study time. I am learning to avoid this. I noticed that when I study for a class I'm going to teach, I focus on a more generalized application. I am not as focused on *personal* application. In this scenario, the application is generated by the person, but it is not as much for the person.

God tends to send me a little nudge (I doubt with His elbow) when I do this. I recall times preparing for a class and thinking the research I had uncovered would be helpful for the people in the class. This is paramount to *me* giving *them* an elbow in the ribs. Thankfully, a little thought invades my brain and takes over my study time. This little thought usually centers on the idea that I might need to learn this passage and apply it to myself before I ever present it to others. I know this for sure: The lessons I teach where I have applied personal action to personal study are much easier for me to present.

***Thank you, God. Message received.***

In the beginning, it was suggested to begin study in prayer. As you ask God to direct your study, I think it is a good idea to ask God to show you the ways He would have you apply personal action to your personal study of His word.

## ——— IT'S YOUR TURN. ———

The application I presented above has a bit of a personal flair to it, but let's attempt to make it even more personal. Expand on your specific application and see what you might do to make it more personal. What personalized action could you implement from your work in Matthew 11:28–30? Write it in the box below.

Here is what I came up with for my specific and personal application:

> "*What if* I stop when I feel unappreciated at work—before I let it affect me? What if I stop and rest from my frustration? What if I focus on solutions I could implement to help me eliminate my frustration?

Notice the personal ownership of my feelings and the attempt at personal solutions. My thoughts and feelings are the only focus of this application. Count the times *I*, *my*, and *me* are used. I am not focused on others. This is a personal application.

## Applications Are Attainable

> "What if the next time I felt unappreciated at work, I bought the company and fired everyone who irritated me?"

For most of us, this would likely not be an attainable application. While some who read this application may consider it with a wry smile, I will take this moment to point out that applications should be constructive and positive. Sorry to burst your bubble. Developing an application that can actually be attained is the next feature of a useful application.

If I set a goal to spend more time learning God's Word, I wouldn't set an application to read the entire Bible each day for a year. I could not physically attain this. I probably couldn't read the entire Bible all the way through in a week, so I would need to consider what is truly attainable for me. What if I committed to reading God's Word from 7:00 a.m. to 8:00 a.m. every morning? This would be much more attainable.

## ——— IT'S YOUR TURN. ———

What language could we use to further develop the application we have been working on? Expand on your specific and personal application and add language that ensures it is attainable. Write this in the box.

Here is my idea:

> "What if the next time I felt unappreciated at work, I stopped for five minutes and quietly went to Jesus in prayer and rested in His promise? What if, during that time, I tried to define exactly why I felt unappreciated? What if I quit working alone and accepted the yoke from God to help me find different ways to work through the situation?"

Taking five minutes for prayer, rest, and reflection is all attainable. We are on the right track. Let's check the boxes for the progress of our application so far. A five-minute break is both specific and attainable. Check. A focus on the rest in Matthew 11:28 is specific to what I studied and learned. Check. The use of

*I* and *me* instead of *you* and *them* keeps my application personal. Check. Teaming up with God to find different ways to work aligns specifically with what I learned in Matthew 11:29. Check.

Check it out. We are getting there. There is just one feature of application left to consider.

## Applications Are Measurable

All my woodworking and construction friends say to me, "Measure twice, cut once." If you have ever ruined a piece of lumber by cutting it too short, you understand this phrase. I would not call myself a carpenter, but I have made a few attempts at completing woodworking projects. There have been times when I did not properly measure. The unmeasured action of cutting ruined my material, and this is why there are unfinished projects in my garage.

The ability to measure an application allows me to know I have accomplished something in my study. If that sounds vital, it's because it is. If I can't measure the application, my study is probably not finished. Finish up your application by adding language that makes it measurable so you know what you have accomplished in your study. Write this in the box below.

Here is my measurable application:

"What if for a period of one month, I stopped when
I began to feel unappreciated at work? What if I qui-
etly took five minutes each time this occurred, and
I went to Jesus in prayer and rested in His promise?
What if next week, I quit working alone and accepted
the His yoke and instruction as I consider solutions
to my frustration? What if, for the rest of the month,
I engage in my employment, trusting that He is with
me as I work? What if I documented the events of the
month in a journal?

I can measure the period of one month mentioned
in the first line of this application. I can measure the
five minutes of quiet prayer. I can measure the next
week accepting Jesus's yoke. Finally, I can measure
trusting and writing in a journal for a month. We
have done more than *measure twice cut once*. We
have measured multiple times. Notice how mea-
surement helps with the development of an effective application.

NOTE: Most of my applications are shorter than the
ones I have provided in this chapter. These are longer
because I was illustrating a point. There isn't a con-
crete rule here. Your application should be as long or
as short as needed for it to be effective. I will just offer
that most of my applications are a single sentence.

## Application Summary

We have taken the four features of application and formed actions based on our study. The next time you study a passage, consider the features of application as you finish up your study. Make them specific so you can understand them. Make them personal so *you* can do it. Make them attainable so it is even possible. Make them measurable so you know you've done it. Specific, personal, attainable, and measurable applications provide direction and focus to our study. Engage them in your future study and see what happens in your life.

## A Final "What If"

Here's another "what if." What if you read through an entire method of studying the Bible? What would happen when you got to the last part of the method? Would you feel good that you invested the time in reading it?

We have read passages multiple times. We have discovered and documented observations. We have collected grammatical and historical evidence to support and explain our observations. We took time to contemplate the implication and rationale surrounding our observations and answered *The Basic Question* in a condensed summary. Finally, we designed specific, personal, attainable, and measurable actions to apply *The Basic Question* in our lives. We have put significant effort into this passage. There is more to learn in this passage, but hopefully, the *Bible Study Lab* method and this trip through portions of Matthew have impacted your life. I know it has mine. Thanks for taking the journey with me.

I have one last thing to share with you. Turn the page, and I'll tell you a story as we finish up.

Bible Study Lab

# Method Development 10 (Final Summary)

- Begin study by recognizing the Bible is not written to me. This leads me to consider *The Basic Question:* "What did this mean to the original reader or audience?"
- **Prepare for Study:** Clear your mind and pray before starting any study. Choose the online or print resources you prefer.
- **The Actions of Study:**
  1) **Read:** Read a passage until you have thoroughly observed the scenery in it. Consider the unit of measure and read the entire book if possible. At a minimum, find the beginning and end of the passage using grammatical pointers. Ask simple questions or read an introduction to the book from your resources to help with reading focus. Roll the throttle back, release the busyness of life, and let the scenery come to you. Take as much time as it takes.
  2) **Observe:** Engage the "hmmms" in your reading. As you read, your intellectual curiosity will point you to features that may need attention. An observation remains a random thought or question until it is documented.

a. Grammatical features, such as word definitions, parts of speech, mood, tense, and word study, are important.

b. The two keys of observation are *grammar* and *history*. Determine which key applies to your observation and consult the online or print resources to gather the evidence to support or explain it.

c. Grammatical evidence is given. Historical evidence is gathered over time. The three categories of history are people, places, and practices. Watch for the categories as you read and observe. Understand the people, find the places, and learn the practices. Gather as much detail as you can in each category.

3) **Interpret:** Contemplate the gathered evidence and consider the implications and rationale of your observations as you prepare to answer *The Basic Question*.

4) **Apply:** Attach action and purpose to your study. There are four features of an application. Applications are specific, personal, attainable, and measurable.

*Chapter 10*

# The Big Finish?

My wife and I took a trip with six of our friends to stay in a beautiful mountain home nestled in the middle of Crested Butte, Colorado. It was my first real stay in the mountains during the summer. It won't be the last. The idea was to relax, enjoy the scenery and our friends, and then relax some more. Oh yeah, and then we relaxed. Sound good? It was awesome.

The morning temps were in the low forties, but you could sit on the patio in shorts and a T-shirt and enjoy a cup of coffee. The morning sun would cover you like a blanket, keeping you warm and comfortable. The afternoon temps were in the seventies. It was perfect to be outside, and we took advantage of it. Life slowed down. We walked all over Crested Butte and hiked the not-so-little trails around it. We shopped in fresh produce markets and unique little stores. We ate like there wasn't going to be food available for the next day. In the evenings, we sat around a large farmhouse table, talked, and played cards. The entire week was exactly what I needed.

On our last day, we hiked up into the mountains. We drove out of town, past the ski resort, and beyond the riding stables. Eventually, the paved roads stopped, and we crossed a cattle guard in the road. This told me we were about to become remote. That assessment was correct.

We drove on high cliff-side dirt roads through mountain scenery and wildlife to reach the place where we could park the truck. It was stunning. There were majestic mountaintops all around us. A cold mountain stream made its way around massive rocks that had fallen off the mountain and into its path. It was one of those "try to tell me God doesn't exist, and I will laugh at you" kinds of places.

When we arrived, we got out of the truck, stretched a bit, and headed up the mountain on our hike. Along the way, we occasionally passed some folks on the trail. Some were walking down the mountain, looking a little less than fresh. Some stopped as if they were enjoying the view, but they were panting like dogs on a hot summer day. I realized they weren't viewing as much as they were surviving. I would know why later.

The scenery was powerfully beautiful, so we just kept going up the trail. At first, I didn't think it was a particularly strenuous hike. Soon my legs disagreed. My mind chimed in on the discussion, reminding the rest of me that "what goes up, must come down," but we just kept going up and up and up.

Finally, we got to the top and found some level ground. It wasn't the tiptop of the mountain range, but we had definitely arrived at the top of something, and I was happy. We stopped to catch our breath and take in the view. That little stream we had noticed as we parked was barely even visible from the extreme height we had achieved. We had done it. And I was proud.

A few feet beyond me there was a short trail that appeared to end at a sign. I was physically done, but I had to go read it. After all, the sign was the prize. I had made it to the top. The sign was there for me to read and prove that I had completed the grand expedition. I felt a sense of accomplishment building in me as I headed for the sign. What would it say? "Congratulations, you did it"? Would it provide some mountaintop wisdom? A few more steps up, and I would know. My legs begged me to stop. My lungs threatened to quit the team, but I just kept going. I thought about crawling the last few steps to increase the dramatic effect, but I restrained myself. When I arrived, I looked at the sign. Here is what I saw:

"Welcome to the trailhead. Enjoy your hike."

Yep. After all that "up", after exhausting all of our personal resources, we had merely found the starting point of the hike. I looked around, hoping this was a practical joke. As I did, I noticed that just behind us was a hidden, primitive parking lot with a few four-wheel-drive vehicles in it. In other words, we could have driven to this spot. In more other words, we weren't on a trail at all. Our entire grand expedition had merely been the road to get to the trail!

At this point, I have something to tell you, dear reader.

"Welcome to the trailhead. Enjoy your hike."

Normally, authors tie everything together and end a book with a big finish and everybody walks away satisfied that the story is over. This book doesn't work like that. It can't because we've just been on the road *to get to the hike*. But now, it's time to get on the trail. Just like my big hike, the seemingly big finish of this book turns out to be the trailhead of your journey.

We have learned about the importance of study techniques. When we read, we should forget about the schedule and use intellectual curiosity to see the scenery around us. As we look around, we observe things in the text we are reading and write them down. This is where it gets interesting. We take our observations and determine whether a specific observation is grammatical in nature or historical in nature, or both. Then we go to the resources and gather the evidence. Once we have our evidence, we ask implicational and rational questions to help us fully understand what the passage would have meant to the original reader or audience. When we understand this, we are ready to develop an application for our own lives. This is Bible study. This is the actual hike.

That day on the mountain, people who were coming off the actual trail encouraged us to keep going. They told us the effort was worth it. They were right. It was worth it. The result of our continued effort was a beautiful waterfall high on the mountain. The waterfall fell into a canyon and roared all the way down the mountainside to the valley below. It ultimately fed into that little stream we had seen when we arrived. A sign had been erected there that gave us the history of what had happened at that site. The beauty of that spot and its accompanying history were undoubtedly worth the effort to get there.

In a similar—OK, almost the exact way—I offer you encouragement as you stand at the trailhead of Bible study. Please keep going because it is worth it. I can't tell you what you will see, but I know it will be beautiful and powerful and you will be glad you are there. Keep going. When it seems like you can't take another step, read another verse or consult another resource. Talk to God as you go. Tell Him your struggles. Share your confusion with Him. Ask Him to show you what He would have you see. He is your Friend. He is your Creator. He knows you can do it, and He is ready to take the journey with you. Just keep going.

"Welcome to the trailhead.
I can't wait to hear your story . . ."

www.biblestudylab.com

# Acknowledgments

Thank you, Dad. When I was a kid, every day, you told me, "I'm proud of you, son. I believe in you; you can do anything you set your mind to doing." You believed in me and made sure I knew it. I still hear your words as an adult. They are invaluable to me.

Thank you, Mom, for sewing into me the thread of what you believed to be honest and true. Your attention to detail was truly beyond my capacity, but some of it stuck, and I am a better man and writer because of it.

Thank you to the people of Crossings Community Church who attended classes on the early versions of *Bible Study Lab*. These classes had so much information that they were less like drinking from a fire hydrant and more like drinking from the city water tower. Your patience helped bring *Bible Study Lab* to its current version.

Thank you to Skip McKinstry, Larry Harrison, Brent and Debi Stockwell, and the staff at Crossings Community School, who all invested themselves in this manuscript before it was a published work. You were the first to see it. As a first-time author, it was petrifying to put this in your hands. You provided the grace I needed in what was the most difficult part of writing to me.

Thanks to Jay Parks, who has always believed in me and made the path to my publisher possible.

Thanks to my editor, Cortney Donelson, for turning my original manuscript into a Jackson Pollock painting so it would be something a human being could read. Thanks to David Hancock and everyone at Morgan James Publishing who took a chance, provided a path, and helped me see the possibilities of my writing.

A special thanks to Dr. Cliff Sanders. This method would not exist without you. You are my friend and mentor. It is hard to express the level of impact you have had on my life and specifically my ability to write this book.

# About the Author

**C**hris Helterbrand has had extensive experience attending, designing, and leading training programs in the medical industry over the last thirty years. Additionally, Chris has been studying the Bible and teaching Bible classes, leading Bible groups, and giving presentations in churches for twenty-five years. For the past decade, together with his mentor, Dr. Cliff Sanders, he has been developing and presenting a unique method called *Bible Study Lab*. This methodology combines Chris's experience in delivering efficient training, his passion for Scripture, and his ambition to help others comprehend the greatest literary work ever created. Chris and his wife Trina are happily settled down in Oklahoma City, Oklahoma.

# A free ebook edition
# is available with the
# purchase of this book.

**To claim your free ebook edition:**

1. Visit MorganJamesBOGO.com
2. Sign your name CLEARLY in the space
3. Complete the form and submit a photo of the entire copyright page
4. You or your friend can download the ebook to your preferred device

**Morgan James BOGO™**

A **FREE** ebook edition is available for you or a friend with the purchase of this print book.

CLEARLY SIGN YOUR NAME ABOVE

**Instructions to claim your free ebook edition:**
1. Visit MorganJamesBOGO.com
2. Sign your name CLEARLY in the space above
3. Complete the form and submit a photo of this entire page
4. You or your friend can download the ebook to your preferred device

## Print & Digital Together Forever.

Snap a photo

Free ebook

Read anywhere

Printed in the USA
CPSIA information can be obtained
at www.ICGtesting.com
JSHW022327280124
56171JS00003B/3